BITTERS & SHRUB SYRUP
COCKTAILS

BITTERS & SHRUB SYRUP
COCKTAILS

Restorative Vintage Cocktails, Mocktails & Elixers

Warren Bobrow

Fair Winds Press
100 Cummings Center, Suite 406L
Beverly, MA 01915

fairwindspress.com • quarryspoon.com

I'm dedicating this book to my grandmother, Sophia Bobrow. For listening to me.

© 2015 Fair Winds Press
Text © 2015 Warren Bobrow

First published in the USA in 2015 by
Fair Winds Press, a member of
Quarto Publishing Group USA Inc.
100 Cummings Center
Suite 406-L
Beverly, MA 01915-6101
www.fairwindspress.com
Visit www.QuarrySPOON.com and help us celebrate food
and culture one spoonful at a time!

19 18 17 16 15   1 2 3 4 5

ISBN: 978-1-59233-675-3

Digital edition published in 2015
eISBN: 978-1-62788-282-8

Library of Congress Cataloging-in-Publication Data available

Book design by The Lincoln Avenue Workshop
Photography by Glenn Scott Photography
Photo styling by Jen Beauchesne

Printed and bound in China

The information in this book is for educational purposes only. It is not intended to replace the advice of a physician or medical practitioner. Please see your health care provider before beginning any new health program.

FOREWORD

I first came to know Warren Bobrow through his spirits writing, specifically his whisk(e)y criticism. His many insightful contributions to SoFAB Institute's former house periodical caught my eye. Then they caught my imagination. Then, the proof in the pudding, as it were, they caught my palate. His prose, ever poetic yet ever clear, is a reader's delight. And the substance of that prose? Taste the subject of one of his articles, or render one of his recipes, and you'll likely be rewarded with a more nuanced understanding of a given brand, expression, or marque, even a longstanding favorite, or deeper appreciation for a classic cocktail, new love for an old flame, if you will.

While I consider myself reasonably adept at assessing the inherent value of a spirit, both neat and cocktailed, Warren's work has expanded my capacity to judge a given spirited beverage's applied value. In *Apothecary Cocktails*, his first book, Warren explored the cocktail's colorful pre-Prohibition past, an era in which beverage manufacturers could make spurious claims about the curative power of their elixirs with impunity, and mined it for equal parts liquid refreshment and modern amusement. Then, with *Whiskey Cocktails*, he rescued lost whiskey-forward recipes and gave readers a new way of approaching brown spirits. In so doing he no doubt converted more than a few avowed whiskey-phobes, those who one could imagine countering the offer of an Old Fashioned with, "Oh, I'm not a whiskey person."

Now, with *Bitters and Shrub Syrup Cocktails*, Warren reaches into the cocktail's protohistory, reveals its forgotten foundations, and reintroduces them to a legion of bartenders eager to know the ancient underpinnings of their craft and a rapidly growing market of enthusiasts hungry, nay, thirsty for more intimate knowledge of the object of their affection, as well as user-friendly home applications of that knowledge.

Finally, as publisher of *SoFAB Magazine*, a beneficiary of his talent and forum for his thoughts on all things imbibed, I look forward to Warren's continued contributions to the field, the literature, and, well, my palate.

—Philip M. Dobard, Vice President
SoFAB Institute, Home of The Museum of the American Cocktail

CONTENTS

Connoisseurs of craft cocktails and mixologists alike owe a major debt of thanks to folk healers of yore. See, back in the day—before refrigerators, antibiotics, and Alka-Seltzer—the only remedies available to early pharmacists were plant based. Since these healing herbs, fruits, and vegetables could spoil easily and quickly, it made sense to preserve them in alcohol or vinegar—that way they could be stored nearly indefinitely.

And that's where bitters and shrubs come in. When we think of bitters, most of us think of that ancient bottle of Angostura that's been shoved to the back of the liquor cabinet since 1982. But what are they, actually? Well, bitters are highly concentrated herb, root, spice, and flower essences combined with some form of distilled alcohol. They were originally used to soothe digestive troubles, circulatory ailments, and to counter the effects of enjoying just a little too much good food and strong drink. And, since home refrigeration wasn't an option until the early twentieth century, kitchen sanitation wasn't what it is today. That means perishable foods spoiled easily, which led to myriad tummy troubles, to put it delicately—and traveling and local apothecaries would have been called upon to provide remedies for sufferers' sore bellies. Even today, a glass of seltzer water doctored up with a couple of dashes of Angostura bitters and a pinch of sea salt is a great natural curative for queasy stomachs.

I'm often asked why bitters are so, um, bitter. Simply put, bitters are made from bitter-tasting herbs and roots. (In days gone by, that would have given a patient confidence in the curative his doctor or pharmacist pre-scribed: Highly astringent medicines were thought to be more effective than their tastier counterparts.) Today, it's that same trademark bitterness that makes them so desirable—but for very different reasons. Bitters have become to cocktail mixologists what seasonings, herbs, and spices are to a chef. They can help to balance the sweet aromatics inherent in some cocktails, adding nuance and mystery to every single sip. Topping a drink with bitters is usually the final step in preparing a cocktail, but once in a while they're used in the first steps of cocktail construction: think of the French 75, for instance, which calls for an Angostura bitters-moistened sugar cube, lemon juice, gin, and champagne. So, even if you're not sure you're a fan of bitters' astringent flavor, chances are you've already had them without even knowing it—and I'll bet you were bewitched by them.

When it comes to bitters, though, less is much, much more. Mixologists never use bitters in excess: They're usually delivered directly to the soul of a cocktail with a medicine dropper. They're highly concentrated, potent flavors, and they're always used sparingly. Same goes for the use of richly flavored, vinegar-based shrubs in mixed drinks. Shrubs are flavorful mixtures of vinegar and sugar, and their name derives from the word "shurb," which, in turn, is from the Arabic for "to drink." (Sherbet, the frozen concoction of ice and fruit flavors, is also a derivative of "shurb.") Don't be misled by the name: Just like money, shrubs don't grow on trees, so there's no point scrabbling around the bushes in your back yard in hopes of finding the ingredients for that cocktail you're craving. Most shrubs are made with three essential ingredients: vinegar; a sweetener, such as sugar, honey, or maple syrup; and fruits and/or vegetables that have been preserved or acidulated by vinegar. Like bitters, vinegar has been touted as a digestive aid for hundreds, if not thousands, of years, since consuming vinegar may help eliminate toxins from the digestive tract. Which means this magic threesome could soothe your belly, deliver a wallop of much-needed vitamins, *and* put a little pep in your step—all at the same time.

Shrubs truly were the original energy drinks, and they were super-popular during the nineteenth and early twentieth centuries. These early shrubs consisted of little more than a sweetening agent, like honey or sugar, combined with water and vinegar, but that simple combination of sweet, tart, and savory makes for a really refreshing, revitalizing beverage. Thirst-slaking shrubs were the soft drinks of their era, before fizzy, highly sugared soda pop exploded onto the world stage.

Today, shrubs have captured the attention of top mixologists, many of whom are interested in how cocktail history can be reinvented and re-imagined in contemporary craft cocktails. Professional mixologists and home bartenders alike are attracted by shrubs' deep, concentrated flavors and their funky, sweet-tart aromatics. The best part is, shrubs are easy to make at home. Just about any type of fruit or vegetable you can think of can be made into a shrub—and, while there are usually several steps in the shrub-making process, it's actually pretty simple. In the chapters to follow, I provide full recipes for each of my shrubs, of course, but the process generally goes like this: Fruits or vegetables are combined with sugar or simple syrup and spices in a nonreactive bowl. After leaving them to sit for about twenty-four hours in order to promote natural fermentation, the fruit-sugar mixture is crushed or pressed to release the intensely flavored juices. Then the juices are mixed with vinegar and left to sit for up to several weeks to combine. The result? A concentrated, flavorful "liqueur" that adds layers of character to each sip of your homemade cocktails.

That's not to say that bitters and shrubs are for bar use only. Bring them straight into the kitchen, because they're delicious in savory and sweet dishes alike. In my recipe for Broiled Grapefruit with Palm Sugar, Brandy, and Angostura Bitters, broiled grapefruit—a breakfast-time treat that hails from the Caribbean islands—gets prettied up with a crackly, "brûléed" crust of caramelized sugar, a hit of brandy, and a dash of palate-tickling Angostura bitters. And, when you boil a shrub so that it continues to reduce, you get an intensely flavored sauce called a *gastrique* that adds spikes of flavor to whatever's on the menu. If that happens to be my Vietnamese-style Chicken Scaloppini with Tea Gastrique, you'll simmer up a *gastrique* of Lapsang

Souchong tea, cane sugar, lemon juice, and cider vinegar that's the perfect tangy-sweet complement to boneless chicken breast dusted in panko crumbs and sautéed with Vietnamese seasonings (or shallot, garlic, onion, and herbs, if you'd rather).

But first, let's mix up a cocktail. If you're ready to go shrubbing, my Lime and Ginger Shrub is a great place to start. Here, limes, fresh ginger, brown sugar, and apple cider vinegar combine to produce toothsome syrup that's a natural match for rum and salty lemonade. Or, if you just can't wait that long, try an English Pea and Mint Shrub. Ready to use in just 36 hours, its fresh, delicate taste takes center stage in the Last Minute Rumpus—a cocktail that bolsters the shrub with white rum, cool spring water, sarsaparilla bitters, lime, and a scraping of nutmeg. After you stir up my Raw Honey Aromatic Bitters, you'll have the needful for the Jimmy Gillespie Fizz, a minimalist combination of Scotch, lemon peel, bitters, and just a dash of spring water. (Take my word for it: it's the best cure for that self-inflicted sore belly and head.) If you prefer to skip the booze and keep the flavor, look no further than my Cucumber and Basil Shrub. It's the main ingredient in the Mr. Rankeillor's Door mocktail, and, with its sea salt, seltzer, and a dash of your homemade Raw Honey Aromatic Bitters, it's the last word in refreshing. For your next weekend brunch, serve your guests a round of my Askew Bloody Marys, where vodka loses out in favor of tequila, and celery bitters replace plain old Worcestershire.

Oh, and one final word before you start mixing: Treat your homemade shrubs and carefully crafted cocktails right by always mixing them with top-quality ingredients. Don't mask your shrubs and fine liquors with artificial mixers and sugar-laden juices: instead, use freshly squeezed, preferably organic fruit juices. And always make your own ice: use spring water, not chlorinated tap water, and double-boil it before freezing it. I hand-cut my ice as much as possible, but when I can't, I use the silicone ice-cube trays that can easily be found in specialty shops or online. It requires a little extra effort, but it's worth it: The quality of your ice really

does make a difference in the way your cocktails will taste. The moral of the story is, with just a bit of patience and know-how, you can usually make better-quality ingredients for your cocktails at home than you can buy in any shop or supermarket.

Once you know how to make and use them, bitters and shrubs are a great way to add distinction and character to fine handmade cocktails (and food, too). Let's get started!

Thirsty drinkers have been enjoying shrubs for centuries, and today, they're absolutely essential to any craft mixologist's bag of tricks. That's because they combine vinegar's tangy acidity with sugar's mellow sweetness, creating broad, bold brush-strokes of flavor that can make your handcrafted cocktails shine.

And shrubs have been hailed as powerful digestive aids since time immemorial.

Before refrigeration became widespread, and before the Pure Food and Drug Act of 1906, foods that weren't pickled, salted, or smoked went bad very quickly, so food poisoning and other belly-based maladies ran rampant. Consuming small amounts of vinegar helped to gently cleanse and recalibrate the sufferer's digestive system.

That's not the only reason shrubs were so valuable to generations past. Like bitters, shrubs can preserve fragile ingredients through the use of controlled fermentation: that is, by extracting flavor from fruit or vegetable ingredients with sugar, then ceasing the fermentation by adding vinegar. Seamen would have mixed a shrub very similar to my Ginger-Lime Shrub with a little water and a heavy dose of rum to stave off scurvy. Fresh fruits and vegetables would have rotted quickly during the long weeks at sea, but by preserving their essences through controlled fermentation in shrubs, sailors could avoid the painful disease. Later, shrubs became a key ingredient in rum punch: a hearty dollop of shrub syrup would have been added to a mixture of rum and water—an extremely popular beverage with gentlemen of the eighteenth century.

Lots of the recipes for shrubs in this chapter have their roots in colonial America, when nearly everything Americans ate or drank would have been produced on their local farms. Shrubs can be made from just about anything: citrus fruits, berries, stone fruits, rhubarb, peas, beets, carrots, peppers, onions—you name it. And there's nothing complicated about making shrubs. Just as it would have been for your eighteenth-century ancestors, the most important ingredient in a shrub is patience, since some of the best shrubs can take a month, or even longer, to prepare. (Never fear, though: there are plenty of shrubs that can be whipped up in mere minutes. Check out chapter 2 for the recipes!)

Before you go shrubbing, though, go shopping. If you're making a fruit-based shrub, it's worth visiting your local organic greengrocer and asking her or him for fruits that are a bit bruised or are just past their acceptable shelf life. Overripe fruits are perfect for building a handcrafted shrub: since their sugar concentration is high, they'll deliver the concentrated flavors and aromatics that'll make your shrub intensely, vibrantly tasty. If you're making a vegetable-based shrub, just be sure to buy the best-quality organic produce you can find.

Then, invest in a couple varieties each of vinegar and sugar. The acidity in shrubs always comes from vinegar, whether it's Japanese rice wine vinegar, balsamic vinegar, apple cider vinegar, or champagne vinegar. Each variety will subtly alter the shrub's flavor profile, as will your choice of sugar. Using white sugar, muscovado sugar, raw honey or maple syrup will add nuance to your shrubs. (Feel free to experiment!) Thanks to the triumvirate of fruit, sugar, and vinegar, shrubs are capable of quenching thirst, stimulating appetite, and curing a stomachache—all at the same time.

Once your shrub is ready, another decision awaits you: What do you drink it with? Start with rum. Lots of the shrub cocktails in this chapter feature handmade white rum from the Caribbean islands, known as *Rhum Agricole,* where the residents are expert shrub makers. (You'll notice that my *Rhum Agricole*-based cocktails in this chapter spell "shrubb" with two "b"s,

in the traditional Caribbean way, while "rum" is spelled with an "h": in rum parlay, "Rhum" signifies an *appellation d'origine contrôlée (AOC)*, or "controlled designation of origin," which means that your bottle of Rhum has met certain standards of production, and will always be made from freshly cut sugarcane instead of the ubiquitous molasses.) You'll find that clear spirits such as gin or vodka work well, too, as evidenced by the Squire's Shrub Cocktail: It's a combination of gin, lemon bitters, and a dose of a toothsome Strawberry-Rhubarb Shrub. And don't forget that shrubs are valuable allies in the kitchen as well. When reduced over high heat into a concentrated sauce called a *gastrique,* they can give dishes a unique sweet-sour edge. (Find out more about how to cook with shrubs in chapter 7.)

But first, it's time to get your shrub on. If you're a first-timer, start with the ridiculously simple Ginger-Lime Shrub. It calls for only four ingredients, which you probably have on hand already—limes, Demerara sugar, fresh ginger, and apple cider vinegar—and it's at its best in a batch of Scurvy Knave Punch, a powerful mixture of rum, sparkling wine, citrus, and a few liberal dashes of bitters. Or, for a shrub with a savory-sweet edge, try my Nectarine, Celery, and Black Pepper Shrub. You'll be surprised at how well celery sets off the lush, summery flavors of fresh nectarines—and you'll be aching to try my Captain John Silver's Nectarine-Celery Fizz. White rum, yellow chartreuse, a couple ounces of the nectarine-based shrub, and a hit of seltzer make it an incredible restorative for flagging palates.

This chapter is packed with my favorite shrub recipes, but there's no such thing as right or wrong when it comes to flavor combinations. Feel free to use my recipes as guidelines, and to take risks: use a different kind of sugar here, a different type of vinegar there, or substitute one variety of fruit or vegetable with another. After all, creativity and experimentation are at the very heart of excellent mixology.

GINGER-LIME SHRUBB WITH *RHUM AGRICOLE* AND SALTY LEMONADE

THIS EASY-TO-MAKE BUT *very grown-up glass of lemonade also showcases that classic ginger-lime-rum combination. I make mine with a healthy portion of 100-proof* Rhum Agricole *(which, if drunk on its own, is guaranteed to put hair on your eyeballs).* Rhum Agricole *is handmade on the French island of Martinique, and it's never factory-produced, which is why I prefer it. But, in a pinch, any good white rum will do. Add a toothsome crunch to your lemonade by sprinkling a little* fleur de sel, *or sea salt, into it. The salt-lemon combination will make you thirsty, but the sugar and vinegar in the shrubb syrup will quench your thirst in double time. This cocktail makes a great summertime aperitif. Mix up a batch at your next barbeque.*

2 tablespoons (30 ml)
Ginger-Lime Shrub
(see page 20)

2 ounces (60 ml) 100-proof
Rhum Agricole Blanc

3 ounces (90 ml)
freshly made lemonade
sweetened with raw
honey or simple syrup

1/2 ounce (15 ml)
seltzer water

1 pinch *fleur de sel*

2–3 drops lime bitters

hand-cut ice spear

Add the Ginger-Lime Shrub to an old fashioned glass. Then add the ice spear. Top with the Rhum Agricole Blanc, the lemonade, and a splash of seltzer water. Sprinkle a pinch of *fleur de sel* into the drink, and finish with a couple drops of lime bitters. It's ridiculously refreshing.

GINGER-LIME SHRUB

IT'S LIKELY THAT A VERSION *of this luscious shrub would have been served aboard sailing ships in days of yore, so that thirsty sailors could escape scurvy. Fragile citrus fruit wouldn't have lasted long, but luckily, the apple cider vinegar in this recipe acts as a powerful preservative. These days, a Ginger-Lime Shrub is a flavorful addition to dozens of cocktails—especially ones involving rum. Hard to starboard, lads!*

peeled zest of 4 well-washed limes (discard the pith: it's very bitter)

4 limes (reserve the ones from the zest), quartered

1 cup (200 g) Demerara sugar

6 tablespoons (48 g) freshly grated ginger root

1–2 cups (235–475 ml) apple cider vinegar (depending on the height of the ingredients when placed in a bowl)

TIME: 3–4 WEEKS. In a nonreactive bowl, combine the lime peels, lime chunks, sugar, and the ginger. Stir to combine and coat all the fruit with sugar. Cover and leave at room temperature at least overnight or for 1–2 days. (Slow, cool fermentation gives a shrub its trademark bite.) Now prepare your shrub for aging. Set a strainer over another nonreactive bowl and pour the lime and ginger into the strainer. Use a stout wooden spoon to extract as much juice as possible from the limes and the softened ginger. Let the mixture sit for a few more hours. Stir again, and discard the fruit chunks. Stir in the vinegar, and then use a funnel to transfer the shrub syrup to a sterilized bottle. Seal, and then shake well to combine. Store the bottles in the refrigerator or at cellar temperature for 3–4 weeks before using. Shake each bottle once or twice daily to help the sugar dissolve. When it's mostly dissolved, your shrub is ready to use. Makes 1 1/2 cups. Keep refrigerated, and use within about 6 months. (If the bottle gets foamy, changes radically in color, or if you suddenly notice small sea animals gorging themselves on thin wafers inside the bottle, just throw it out. If you don't tell anyone about the thin wafers or the sea animals, I promise I won't tell anyone, either.)

BACK IN THE AGE OF SAIL, *vitamin C–laden fruits, like lemons and limes, were precious cargo: They could keep seagoing men from contracting scurvy, a painful and often fatal disease. Ship cooks would boil lime juice, ginger root, sugar, and vinegar until they formed a thick syrup that, coincidentally, was delicious when mixed with rum. That way, sailors could get a dose of much-needed vitamin C—with a bit of a kick. Use the best rum you can afford: if you use poor-quality industrial-grade rum, you'll feel more than a little seasick the next morning. (And your guests will be wont to give you a bath in the warm bilge water inside the keel of your ship.) A "Scurvy Knave" is a less-than-sympathetic term for someone in the throes of the disease, but don't worry: a cup or two of this potent punch is a sure cure.*

4 ounces (120 ml) dark rum

4 ounces (120 ml) light rum

4 ounces (120 ml) overproof rum

6 ounces (175 ml) Ginger-Lime Shrub (see opposite)

1 750 ml bottle of sparkling wine

10 shakes Peychaud's Bitters

1 jobo fruit (or 1 tangerine)

Combine the rum, Ginger-Lime Shrub, and sparkling wine in a large punch bowl. Add the Peychaud's Bitters. Lovingly break open the jobo fruit or tangerine and, using your fingers, squeeze its aromatic flesh into the cocktail. Mix well and serve. This is a punch of memorable proportions and serves at least 5 knaves.

DR. ARROW'S STRONG WATER SHRUB

THIS HISTORIC SHRUB *also takes its inspiration from the Eastern European flavors of Manhattan's Lower East Side. Dr. Arrow's Strong Water Shrub transforms lemons, spices, pickled beets, sugar, and vinegar into syrup that's fragrant, intense, and intoxicating. It's a fabulous match for clear spirits like vodka or gin, so skip that plain old gin-and-tonic for once, and doctor your drink up with a little Strong Water. Remember, vinegar is great for the digestive system, and this savory shrub will have you healthy as a handsome goat in no time.*

4–5 lemons, well washed and peeled (remove as much bitter pith as you can from the peels, then reserve them)

1 cup (200 g) Demerara sugar

1 teaspoon each sweet pickling spices, such as Chinese five star pods, coriander, cloves, cardamom, and/or 1 cinnamon stick

1 pound (455 g) beets, oven-roasted for an hour at 400°F (200°C, or gas mark 6) in foil until soft, cooled, and peeled under water

1 cup (235 ml) rice wine vinegar

TIME: 2–3 WEEKS. Quarter the peeled lemons, and place them in a nonreactive bowl with their peels. Add the sugar, the assorted spices, and the cooked, peeled beets. Stir well to cover the beets and lemons with the sugar. Cover tightly and let sit at room temperature for 24 hours. Mash as much pulp as you can from the lemons and beets, and then strain the liquid from the mixture. Add the vinegar to the liquid, and let sit tightly covered either in the fridge or in a cool, dark place for 2–3 weeks. Funnel your shrub to sterilized bottles, and be sure to shake them every 1–2 days.

DR. ARROW'S STRONG WATER ELIXIR

WONDERING WHAT TO DO *with that batch of Dr. Arrow's that's been aging happily in your fridge? Start with a Strong Water Elixir. We've got beetroot to thank for the bright red hue of this savory cocktail, which tastes as good as it looks. Plus, beets are nutritional powerhouses, full of compounds that may prevent liver and cardiovascular disease—and that, as the saying goes, can't do any harm and may do some good. The Strong Water Elixir makes an excellent aperitif, especially in the winter, when your palate needs a lift before it tackles comfort foods like short ribs, garlic smashed potatoes, and root vegetables. Fresh dill, a twinkling of* fleur de sel, *and a lemon zest twist keep things light and fresh: So go on, have another.*

3 ounces (90 ml) good-quality vodka

4 ounces (120 ml) Dr. Arrow's Strong Water Shrub (see opposite)

2 ounces (60 ml) seltzer

2–3 shakes lemon bitters

lemon zest twists

2 sprigs fresh dill

Pinch of *fleur de sel*

Add the vodka and the shrub to a cocktail mixing glass. Mix gently and use a Hawthorne strainer to divide the mixture between two coupe glasses. Top each glass with 1 ounce (30 ml) of seltzer, and 2–3 shakes of lemon bitters. Garnish each glass with a lemon zest twist and a sprig of fresh dill. Finish each drink with a pinch of *fleur de sel*. Serves two.

BASED ON A NINETEENTH-CENTURY *recipe, it's easy to see why this cherry-based shrub has stood the test of time. Tart, puckery cherries sweeten up by being macerating in a coating of sugar or honey before being mixed with two kinds of vinegar, and the result is a flavorful syrup that's wonderful when paired with whiskey or dark rum; used in place of* crème de cassis *in a Kir Royale; or simply mixed into a tall glass of fizzy water (sweetened with a little raw honey or simple syrup, if you like). So grab your axe and start chopping cherries.*

1 cup (150 g) tart cherries, pitted and chopped

1 cup (340 g) raw honey or (200 g) Demerara sugar

1/2 cup (120 ml) Japanese rice wine vinegar

1/2 cup (120 ml) sweetened Japanese mirin vinegar

TIME: 3–4 WEEKS. Place the cherries in a nonreactive bowl, cover them with the raw honey or sugar, and stir well to coat. (If using raw honey, you may need to warm it to make it easier to spoon over the fruit.) Cover the bowl with plastic wrap, and let it sit at room temperature for 24 hours. Watch the magic happen: Within a few hours the fruit will begin to release its juices. Crush the cherries with a wooden spoon—just like in the old days—then strain them through a nonreactive sieve and add the vinegars to the liquid. Mix well, let the mixture sit for a few hours, and then funnel it into sterilized bottles or Mason jars. Seal the bottles or jars tightly, and age in the fridge for 3–4 weeks. Shake the bottles each day or so. Great in a variety of cocktails and mocktails.

COIL OF STOUT ROPE WHISKY COCKTAIL

DIDN'T I TELL YOU THAT *whisky is the perfect partner for the Coil of Stout Rope Cherry Shrub? I wasn't making it up. Here, smoky, peaty Scotch whisky is swirled with the sweet-and-tangy cherry shrub, and the flavors practically leap from the glass. Finishing with a couple drops of my aromatic raw honey bitters adds extra depth and concentration to this simple-to-make craft cocktail. This peaty, cherry-tinged tipple is the last word in elegance, so go all out and use hand-cut ice instead of run-of-the-mill cubes (or, heaven help us, the store-bought kind): It'll take the Coil from the mundane to the truly sublime. Enjoy it on its own—or with nothing more than a handful of roasted, spiced cashews.*

lemon zest twist

hand-cut ice cube

2 ounces (60 ml) extra-smoky Scotch whisky

2 ounces (60 ml) Coil of Stout Rope Cherry Shrub

1–2 drops water (tap water is fine)

4 drops Cocktail Whisperer's Raw Honey Aromatic Bitters (see page 62) or Quick Raw Honey Bitters (see page 155)

sprig of thyme

Rub the inside of a rocks glass with the lemon zest twist, and then drop the zest into the bottom of the glass. Add one large cube of hand-cut ice, and top with the whisky. Float the Coil of Stout Rope Cherry Shrub over the top of the whiskey, and add a drop or two of water to the shrub float. Dot with 3–4 drops of my Cocktail Whisperer's Raw Honey Aromatic Bitters or Quick Raw Honey Bitters. Float the sprig of thyme on top. Divine.

THE SQUIRE'S STRAWBERRY-RHUBARB SHRUB

IT'S TRUE, THE SQUIRE'S SHRUB *does require a couple of extra steps, but I promise it's worth your while: Your patience will be rewarded with a lush, crimson-colored syrup that's straight out of the eighteenth century, when America was in its infancy and early pharmacists would have relied on their gardens to supply the basis for their healing tonics. (Rhubarb has been used as a digestive aid for thousands of years.) There's nothing difficult to it, though, beyond a little extra mixing, and roasting your fruit before making the shrub. The vinegar's high acidity cuts through the sumptuous, charred, caramelized flavor of the roasted strawberries and rhubarb, making it a seductive addition to gin, vodka, and rum-based libations.*

2 cups (340 g)
Roasted Strawberries and
Rhubarb (see page 152)

1 cup (200 g)
Demerara sugar

1 cup (235 ml) light
balsamic vinegar

TIME: 3–4 WEEKS. Add the roasted strawberries and rhubarb to a nonreactive bowl. Cover with the sugar, stir to combine, and cover it with plastic wrap. Leave at cool room temperature for 24 hours. Stir frequently during this time to combine as the berries and rhubarb give off their liquid. Place a nonreactive strainer above a second nonreactive bowl, pour the fruit-sugar mixture into the strainer, and use a wooden spoon to mash the mixture in order to release as much liquid as possible. (Reserve the mashed fruit to use in cooking or baking, if you like.) Add the balsamic vinegar to the liquid, stir, and let the mixture sit for a few hours. Funnel into sterilized bottles or jars, and age for 3–4 weeks in the refrigerator. This shrub will last nearly indefinitely, but if it begins to quiver, dance, or speak in foreign languages, throw it out.

THE SQUIRE'S SHRUB COCKTAIL

GET READY TO TRY MY *Cocktail Whisperer's twisted take on the French 75, that classic combination of gin, champagne, lemon juice, and simple syrup. This version is actually a hybrid of the French 75 and the traditional champagne cocktail, which calls for a bitters-moistened sugar cube, brandy, and a heady top of champagne. Fuse the two together, add a healthy whack of tart, fruity Squire's Shrub, and you've got a cocktail that'll make your knees tremble. In the same way that alchemists of old strove to turn base metals into gold, champagne can turn a plain old Tuesday into a full-on, hat-waving celebration. Be sure to keep a bottle on hand so you can whip these up the next time you find yourself hosting an impromptu shindig. Make a few batches of the Squire's, if you dare—just keep that bottle of Fernet Branca on hand for the morning after.*

1 brown sugar cube

Several dashes of lemon bitters

1/2 ounce (15 ml) botanical gin

2 ounces (60 ml) Squire's Strawberry-Rhubarb Shrub (see page 28)

1 1/2 ounces (45 ml) champagne or dry sparkling wine

I long lemon zest twist

Add the sugar cube to a champagne flute, and moisten with the lemon bitters. Then add the gin and the Squire's Strawberry-Rhubarb Shrub, and top with champagne. Garnish with a long lemon zest twist.

Note: To prepare this flute, combine very finely chopped lemon zest and sugar, wet the rim of the glass with lemon, and dip the glass into yellow-colored sugar. Voila!

MAPLE SYRUP SWITCHEL

OKAY, SO IT'S NOT TECHNICALLY *a shrub—but the only difference between a switchel and a shrub is shrubs contain fermented fruit or vegetables, while switchel doesn't. Also known as haymaker's punch, switchel originated in the Caribbean, and quickly became popular in the United States. Thirsty farmers have used it for centuries to stay hydrated while working outdoors. And switchel is definitely making a comeback. Expect to see it behind the bar of your favorite craft cocktail lounge soon. In the meantime, why not make your own? It's ready to use more quickly than most shrubs: After just 24 hours in the fridge, you can strain your switchel into rocks glasses filled with ice and an ounce (30 ml) of either brandy or dark rum. Top with a couple drops of my Cocktail Whisperer's Raw Honey Aromatic Bitters (see page 62), and a little soda water, if you like.*

3 tablespoons (45 ml) apple cider vinegar

4 tablespoons (60 ml) Grade B (or dark amber/cooking) maple syrup

1 tablespoon (8 g) of grated fresh ginger root

1 cup (235 ml) of cool spring water (whatever you do, don't substitute tap water!)

TIME: 24 HOURS. Combine all the ingredients in a sterilized Mason jar. Cover tightly and store in the fridge for at least 24 hours, shaking to combine the ingredients. This lasts for several months in the fridge.

NECTARINE, CELERY, AND BLACK PEPPER SHRUB

DOES THE IDEA OF A *celery-flavored drink make you wince? Keep calm: It's good for you. Celery seed has been used as a pain reliever for thousands of years, and may even help lower blood pressure. Plus, celery-flavored soft drinks have been on the market since the late nineteenth century, so a precedent has definitely been set for this delicious shrub. (That said, celery allergies are no joke, and can be potentially life threatening, so if you happen to have a celery allergy or sensitivity, skip this one.) Nectarine and celery juices are brightened with fresh lime juice and sweetened with simple syrup, then combined with a dose of white balsamic: And in two weeks, you'll have a bracing tonic that's also highly refreshing when used—judiciously—in all sorts of cocktails.*

1 pound (455 g) nectarines, peeled, stones removed

½ cup (120 ml) freshly pressed celery juice

1 cup (200 g) Demerara sugar

3 ounces (90 ml) yellow chartreuse

½ teaspoon black peppercorns

4 limes, peeled and quartered (be sure to remove all the bitter white pith)

pinch of *fleur de sel*

½ cup (120 ml) white balsamic vinegar

½ cup (120 ml) white wine vinegar

TIME: 2 WEEKS. Combine the nectarines with the celery juice, Demerara sugar, yellow chartreuse, peppercorns, lime quarters, and the *fleur de sel* in a nonreactive bowl. Cover and let sit at room temperature for 24 hours. Place a nonreactive strainer over a second nonreactive bowl, and transfer the mixture to the strainer, extracting as much liquid from the nectarines as possible by mashing with a wooden spoon. Discard the nectarines and lime segments or cook into a pot roast. (You may want to strain the liquid through two pieces of cheesecloth to remove all the peppercorns: That'll prevent them from getting caught in your teeth later on.) Add both the vinegars and stir. Let the mixture sit for a few hours, and then funnel into sterilized bottles or Mason jars. Store in the fridge and shake daily to help the flavors mellow and combine. After 2 weeks your shrub will be ready to use. Store in the fridge for about 6 months: If it becomes foamy, discard immediately.

CAPTAIN JOHN SILVER'S CELERY-NECTARINE FIZZ

IN ROBERT LOUIS STEVENSON'S *Treasure Island, Captain Silver's men were about to attack and loot a mercantile ship when Silver called to them, "I'm only interested in the wine and the pickles." I couldn't agree more: Who needs hordes of gold and silver bullion when you've got wine and pickles? They taste so much better. There's no wine involved in this Celery-Nectarine Fizz, but there sure are pickles—plus a whole host of exotic, assertive ingredients, like 100-proof hand-crafted white rum, yellow chartreuse (which, incidentally, is created from an ancient recipe of hundreds of flower and plant essences, and was thought to be the key to long life), and lemon bitters. The finishing touch is a scattering of Captain Silver's Quick Celery Pickle, an easy-to-make, 48-hour pickle that makes a crisp, tangy garnish for this memorable cocktail.*

crushed ice

1/2 ounce (15 ml) yellow chartreuse

2 ounces (60 ml) 100-proof *Rhum Agricole Blanc* (or any good 100-proof white rum)

2 ounces (60 ml) Nectarine, Celery, and Black Pepper Shrubb (see page 33)

1 ounce (30 ml) seltzer water

pinch of *fleur de sel*

3 drops lemon bitters

several shards of Captain Silver's Quick Celery Pickle (see page 153)

Fill a coupe glass with water, crushed ice, and the aromatic yellow chartreuse. When the glass is chilled, pour out the chartreuse and water mixture (down your throat, ideally: No need to waste good liquor!) Add the rum to the glass, and pour the shrub over it. Top with the seltzer and a pinch of *fleur de sel*; then add the bitters, garnish with the celery pickle, sip, and lift your glass to the Captain.

"Our patience will achieve more than our force," wrote the eighteenth-century Irish statesman Edmund Burke. He was right—and the same principle applies to making shrubs. Preparing mouthwatering shrubs that'll do your handcrafted cocktails justice does take patience, time, and attention. But what if you just can't wait that long? Fear not: this chapter will show you how to make flavorful shrubs in as little as a few minutes. While it's true that naturally fermented shrubs do benefit from weeks or months in the fridge or cellar—that's how their flavors develop—there are plenty of shrubs you can whip up much more quickly. And that's brilliant news for both professional and home bartenders.

How does the magic happen? Well, you'll notice that lots of the cocktail recipes in this chapter involve a dash of fizzy water or seltzer water. Here's why: the fizzy tang that long fermentation adds to a shrub takes more than a day or two to develop, but adding a dash of bubbly water replaces the missing fizz—and no one will be the wiser. Delicate summer fruits like melon and cantaloupe often work well in quick-shrub recipes, as do autumn and winter fruits like pears, tangerines, limes, lemons, and blood oranges, so you'll be able to create delicious shrubs year-round. And you don't need to stick to fruit, either: Shrubs can be concocted speedily out of fresh, fragrant vegetables, like peas and celery.

Adding vinegar directly to the fruit-and-sugar mixture helps the flavors of quick shrubs, too. That's why some of the recipes in this chapter call for adding the vinegar before you've strained your fruit mixture. It's another way to hurry up the process when there's just no time for your produce to soak in long, cool, soothing vinegar baths. Another way to bring out the flavors of your produce as quickly as possible is to use vinegars with higher levels of acidity. Experiment with a variety of vinegars: This is the perfect opportunity to use that tarragon vinegar you brought back from your trip to France two years ago!

Other secret weapons in the quick-shrubber's arsenal are marmalades and fruit preserves. Since the fruit in preserves has already been cooked and sugared, it's the perfect base for a quick shrub. Once you've got cooked (and sweetened, if necessary) fruit or vegetables on hand, in fact, you can make a good shrub with very minimal *mise en place.* Add a dose of highly acidic vinegar, like a good, strong, unfiltered apple cider vinegar to your cooked fruit, plus a pinch of baking spices, such as nutmeg, cloves, cardamom, or even some cayenne pepper or a Thai chili pepper. Combine with the liquor of your choice in an ice-filled mixing glass: shake, strain into a glass, and finish with some seltzer water to approximate an aged shrub's telltale fizz. Serve, then sit back and watch your guests' faces light up—but be ready to jump up and make another round.

While the recipes in this chapter are for quick shrubs, don't hesitate to age them, if you have time. All my quick-shrub recipes get even better as the days and weeks pass, so if you aren't in a rush, just pop your bottled shrubs into the fridge and be sure to shake them each day or two. After a month or so they'll be aged to perfection—and they'll taste even better than their quickly made counterparts. Plus, they'll last for ages—up to six months—in the fridge, which means you'll be able to enjoy the flavors of lots of seasonal produce at just about any time of the year. (That said, if you notice your shrubs becoming frothy, cloudy with fuzz, or changing significantly in color, do toss them out right away.)

So what are you waiting for? Start making quick shrubs now. Why not begin with my Italian Blood Orange and Charred Rosemary Shrub, which takes just 24 hours from start to finish? It's a potable incarnation of that age-old relationship: citrus and rosemary. And it goes that extra mile: Charring or grilling fruits and vegetables intensifies their flavors, which is why I lightly char my rosemary before adding it to the shrub. Use it alongside excellent bourbon, fizzy water, and grapefruit bitters to make an Assembly Ball Cocktail, an elegant quaff that's a perfect warm-weather aperitif. Can't wait that long, but still crave a drink with a citrus kick? Try the instant version. My Instant Blood Orange Shrub Cocktail takes a major shortcut by using blood orange marmalade, so all the work of sugaring and fermenting the fruit is done for you. A dash of vinegar, some *Rhum Agricole,* and a little fizz, and your "shrub" is done in a matter of minutes. Or, for something on the savory side, try my English Pea and Mint Shrub, which is a great complement to gin. Sweet peas and bracing mint meet champagne vinegar and simple syrup—and the mix is cocktail-ready in only 36 hours. I'll drink to that!

ITALIAN BLOOD ORANGE AND CHARRED ROSEMARY SHRUB

THE COMBINATION OF ORANGE *and rosemary is a match made in heaven, but what sets my Italian Blood Orange Shrub apart from the crowd is its use of charred rosemary, which intensifies the shrub's flavor, and blood oranges, a spunky fruit with blood-red flesh and a taste that lies somewhere between sweet and tart. I beg you to use Italian blood oranges, if you can find them: I think they taste much more authentic than the domestically propagated blood oranges which tend to have fewer seeds. Bound with citrusy yuzu vinegar and Demerara sugar, this shrub can be used in cocktails after just 24 hours. Or, if you've got the patience, you can age it in the fridge or at cellar temperature for a month or two before using it. (Your friends may try to grab a bottle when you're not looking. Just let them try.)*

3–4 blood oranges, prefer-ably Italian ones, peeled (remove as much of the white pith as possible: it's bitter) and quartered. Slice the peel into narrow strips—again, removing as much of the bitter white pith as possible.

1 cup (200 g) Demerara sugar

2–3 stalks of rosemary, held above a flame and *lightly* charred, then cooled

1 cup (235 ml) yuzu vinegar (available at your local Asian market)

TIME: 24 HOURS. Combine the oranges, the peels, sugar, and the charred rosemary (needles only, no wood, please!). Stir to coat the oranges and zest with the charred rosemary. Cover with plastic wrap and let it sit overnight so that the oranges will release their delicious juices. Then add the yuzu vinegar and stir. Let the mixture sit for another 12 hours in the fridge, stirring every hour or so. Then strain the mixture through a nonreactive strainer into a second bowl, pressing as much of the orange pulp through the strainer as possible. Discard the pulp (or serve it alongside fresh scones instead of jam or marmalade). Funnel the liquid into sterilized bottles or jars. Use immediately: or, if you like, leave it in the fridge and forget about it for a month or so, shaking the bottle every so often to combine the sugar, vinegar, and fruit. That'll concentrate the flavors (and intensify the colors) for a particularly lip-smacking shrub.

IT'S TRUE THAT SHRUBS BENEFIT *from time and patience; since the aging process helps their flavors concentrate and improve. But what if your patience just won't hold out? No problem! Shrubs don't have to take forever to make: They can be ready in as little as a few minutes. Take, for example, my Instant Blood Orange Shrubb Cocktail. It's the accelerated version of my Italian Blood Orange Shrub, and it's far quicker, since you don't need to concoct your shrub before you make your cocktail: Instead, you actually make the shrub right into your cocktail. Here, the combination of tart vinegar and club soda's slightly salty effervescence fool your palate into thinking this instant shrub spent weeks aging in the fridge. (And your guests won't know the difference: trust me.) This shrubb cocktail is great with rum, but rye whiskey works just as well. Instant gratification in a glass!*

3 ounces (120 g) blood orange marmalade

1 ounce (30 ml) white balsamic vinegar

1 ounce (30 ml) Basic Simple Syrup (see page 152)

1 ounce (30 ml) 100-proof *Rhum Agricole* or rye whiskey

dash of seltzer water

1–2 shakes orange bitters

TIME: 3–4 MINUTES. Combine the marmalade, vinegar, simple syrup, and rum or rye whiskey over ice in a Boston shaker. Shake like crazy, and then strain into an coupe glass. Top with the seltzer water and the orange bitters. Done.

ASSEMBLY BALL SHRUBB COCKTAIL

AS ELEGANT AS EVENINGWEAR, *this simple citrusy cocktail is a celebration in a glass. It takes its name from the Assembly Ball, a debutante ball first held in Philadelphia in 1748. (Assembly Balls are still held in lots of communities around the country today.) I like to imagine our eighteenth-century ancestors drinking a version of this effervescent cocktail at the event of the season—only, our eighteenth-century ancestors might have used English marmalade or another kind of orange preserves in the absence of easily available fresh oranges. Luckily, you have a batch of my Italian Blood Orange and Charred Rosemary Shrubb ready and waiting. Combine it with the best bourbon you can get, plus a dash of* Rhum Agricole, *grapefruit bitters, and garnish with a piney sprig of rosemary. Serve a round of Assembly Balls as aperitifs at an intimate, late-spring dinner party.*

2 ounces (60 ml) good-quality bourbon

½ ounce (15 ml) 100-proof *Rhum Agricole* (or other good white rum)

2 ounces (60 ml) Italian Blood Orange and Charred Rosemary Shrubb (see page 40)

splash of seltzer water

2–3 drops grapefruit bitters

rosemary sprig, for garnish

Fill a Boston shaker three-quarters full with ice, and pour over the bourbon, the *Rhum Agricole,* and the Italian Blood Orange and Charred Rosemary Shrubb. Cover and shake hard for 15 seconds, and then pour into a coupe glass. Top with the seltzer, and drip 2–3 drops of the grapefruit bitters over the top of the drink. Garnish with a small (non-charred!) sprig of rosemary (try to avoid using too much of the tough, bitter stalk).

COLONIAL SOUR CHERRY SHRUB

GEORGE WASHINGTON HIMSELF *would have agreed that cherries are treasured ingredients when it comes to shrubs. Alas, the growing season is quite short, so if you miss the all-too-brief sour cherry season at your local farm market, never fear: all is not lost. It's easy to make a sour cherry shrub in a hurry if you have a jar of sour cherry preserves on hand. (And you don't have to tell a soul that you cut corners.) Using preserves means you won't have to reduce the fruits over heat; that's already been done for you. This shrub is ready to use in just 36 hours. Or, you can continue to age it in the fridge for up to a month. Don't chuck the lightly fermented cherry-sugar mixture after straining: You can use it to add depth to pork shoulder roasted low and slow, or blended into your mama's corn muffins—best baked in a cast-iron pan, of course.*

1 8-ounce (235-ml) jar of
sour cherry preserves

1 cup (200 g)
Demerara sugar

1 cup (235 ml)
apple cider vinegar

TIME: 36 HOURS. Place the sour cherry preserves in a nonreactive bowl, and cover with the sugar. Let them steep together for at least overnight (or for a few days) at room temperature. Then strain the cherry mixture through a nonreactive sieve, crushing the tender fruits with a wooden spoon to extract as much flavor and sweet juice as possible. Combine with the vinegar; let the mixture sit for a few hours, and then strain and bottle in sterilized bottles. Use the shrub right away, or let it sit in the fridge for three weeks to a month.

NAMED FOR A FORMER CREWMAN *of pirate captain J. Flint in Robert Louis Stevenson's classic novel* Treasure Island, *this cocktail is an homage to Ben Gunn, a sailor who finds himself marooned on Treasure Island for several years. (Weirdly, Gunn also ends up with a monomaniacal craving for cheese.) In the end, though, he discovers Captain Flint's treasure—and you'll feel as lucky as Gunn did when you treat yourself to one of these ambrosial tipples. Rich, jammy Colonial Sour Cherry Shrub marries well with oak-aged dark rum: then, a splash of maple syrup sweetens the deal. Add a little more mystery to your cocktail by making your own maple ice cubes: Combine 1 part maple syrup with 4 parts spring water, and then freeze overnight and hand-cut each cube to order.*

hand-cut ice cube

2 tablespoons (60 ml) Colonial Sour Cherry Shrub (see page 44)

2 ounces (60 ml) dark rum (a molasses-based rum that's been aged in ex-bourbon oak is ideal)

1/4 ounce (7 ml) dark amber (cooking) maple syrup

splash of seltzer water

lemon zest twist

dash of cherry bitters

Place the ice cube in a rocks glass, and add 2 tablespoons (60 ml) of the Sour Cherry Shrub. Add the dark rum and the maple syrup, and then top with a splash of fizzy seltzer water. Garnish with a lemon zest twist, and dot with cherry bitters.

LEMONADE AND BEET JUICE "SHRUB"

THE LOWER EAST SIDE OF *New York City has long been a creative center when it comes to liquid refreshments, and my instant Lemonade and Beet Juice "Shrub" takes its inspiration from a shrub made at Russ and Daughters' Lower East Side delicatessen. Early twentieth-century Eastern European immigrants would have added sweet pickled-beet juice, apple cider vinegar, spices, sugar, and vegetables to tart, homemade lemonade for a healthy, revitalizing quaff. It's an aesthetic treat, too: The beet juice gives the lip-smacking lemonade a bright-red stain. It's darned good, and it's packed with vitamins. My version is booze-free, but if you need a little hair of the dog, add 2 ounces (60 ml) of good-quality vodka. Serve this faux "shrub" with fresh bagels, lox, and cream cheese for brunch.*

1 ounce (30 ml) juice from sweet pickled beets (available at a Kosher deli)

2 ounces (60 ml) Basic Simple Syrup (see page 152)

8 ounces (235 ml) freshly made Homemade Lemonade (see page 152)

pinch of sea salt

3 drops celery bitters

TIME: 5 MINUTES. Fill a Collins glass with crushed ice. Add the beet juice and the simple syrup, and then top with the lemonade and stir. Top with a pinch of sea salt and a couple drops of the celery bitters to finish. A sure cure for whatever ails you!

Shrubs don't need to be fruit-based—and neither do cocktails. Ready in just a day and a half, sweet peas and fragrant mint take center stage in this toothsome shrub that's inspired by your springtime vegetable garden. They're mixed with richly textured Demerara sugar, and then quickly preserved in luxurious champagne vinegar, and the result is a most beguiling, bright-green syrup that's a surprising, refreshing complement to white rum, or even to plain seltzer water. If you can tie yourself to the mast and avoid the shrub's siren call, go ahead and age it in the fridge for a month—but I bet you won't be able to restrain yourself from using it the minute it's ready.

1 pound (455 g) fresh peas, shelled, then blanched (add a pinch of baking soda to boiling water, and then submerge the peas in the water for a few seconds: The baking soda will enhance their vivid green color) and lightly crushed

1 cup (235 ml) Demerara Sugar Simple Syrup (see page 154)

1 cup (235 ml) champagne vinegar

1 cup (95 g) fresh mint, washed and slapped to release its essential oils

TIME: 36 HOURS. Combine the blanched, lightly crushed peas and simple syrup in a nonreactive bowl, and let them sit at room temperature overnight. The next morning, stir the mixture well with a wooden spoon, and then add the champagne vinegar and slapped mint. Stir again, and keep in the fridge for 24 hours so that the flavors combine (be sure to keep your bowl well-covered: You don't want your delicate flavors ruined by that bowl of leftover garlic pasta that lives on the other side of the fridge!). Place a sieve over another nonreactive bowl, and transfer the mixture to the sieve, pressing down so as to extract as much juice from the pea solids as possible. Funnel the mixture into sterilized bottles or jars, and use immediately. Or, let it ferment for up to another month or two in the fridge, shaking the bottles daily so that the sumptuous flavors combine.

LAST-MINUTE RUMPUS

WHY EAT YOUR VEGETABLES *when you could drink them? These days, craft cocktail bars around the country are creating scores of vegetable-based tipples: think pea mojitos or kale margaritas. That's where my Last-Minute Rumpus comes in. This thirst-quencher puts your freshly made batch of English Pea and Mint Shrub to stellar use, and it's nothing more than equal measures of shrub, white rum, and spring water brightened with fresh lime, sarsaparilla bitters, and an appetite-boosting dash of freshly grated nutmeg. Try serving this savory libation alongside a first course, like a simple salad of avocado, citrus, and chopped hazelnuts. Or, indulge in a little daytime drinking, and mix up a Last-Minute Rumpus on one of those late Saturday afternoons when a lazy brunch with a couple of friends stretches right into cocktail hour.*

2 ounces (60 ml) *Rhum Agricole Blanc* **(100 proof)**

2 ounces (60 ml) English Pea and Mint Shrub

2 ounces (60 ml) cool spring water

2 drops sarsaparilla bitters

squeeze of fresh lime juice

scraping of fresh nutmeg

Add the first two ingredients to a rocks glass (no ice necessary). Pour the cool spring water over the top, and mix with your (clean) finger. Add the bitters, followed by the lime juice, and then scrape a little fresh nutmeg into the drink as a final flourish—serve immediately.

ONE EVENING I FOUND MYSELF *sampling a large selection of French* eau de vie—*strong, clear fruit brandy*—*at the New York restaurant Rouge Tomate. One of the many liquors I tried that night was made with*—*count 'em*—*62 different varieties of heirloom tomato. It was intriguing and intoxicating: The haunting tomatoey taste and fragrance infused each sip. Then my thoughts turned to Poire William, an* eau de vie *that's made from impossibly tart pears. What if, I thought, it were possible to combine those tart pears with a portion of the tomato* eau de vie—*combined, say, with a touch of vinegar, crumbled sage, and simple syrup? Stop right there: Before you object, "Where on earth am I going to get tomato* eau de vie?" *I have the answer: Skip the* eau de vie, *and make a batch of my Heirloom Tomato, Pear, and Sage Shrub instead. It's an incredible partner for gin-based cocktails.*

1 cup (255 g) diced heirloom tomatoes

3–4 sage leaves, crumbled

1 cup (235 ml) Bosc Pear "Shrub" Simple Syrup (see page 154)

1 cup (235 ml) apple cider vinegar

TIME: 24 HOURS. Combine the diced tomatoes, sage, and Bosc Pear "Shrub" Simple Syrup in a nonreactive bowl. Stir to combine, then cover the bowl and let the mixture sit at room temperature overnight or for 12 hours. Add the vinegar, stir, cover, and refrigerate for another 12 hours to combine the flavors. Place a nonreactive strainer over a second bowl, and transfer the mixture to the strainer, pressing down on the tomato-sage pulp to extract as much flavor as possible. Funnel into sterilized bottles or jars, and use immediately— or, store in the fridge for a month to let the flavors combine.

GRILLED TANGERINE SHRUB

It's incredibly easy to make quick shrubs when you have plenty of citrus fruit on hand —especially during the winter months, when oranges, tangerines and the like are widely available and so reasonably priced (and when your immune system is probably craving a little vitamin C). That means you've got no reason not to make this delectable 48-hour shrub! I like to grill my tangerines first to add a bit of char to their bright acidity. Then I coat them in simple syrup before combining them with yuzu vinegar, that Japanese kitchen staple—and a day later they're ready for use in cocktails. And being in a hurry doesn't mean your shrub's nuanced flavors have to suffer: It really doesn't take long to bring out the best in hardy, versatile tangerines.

10 small tangerines, peeled and halved, and seared in a cast-iron pan, then cooled, segmented and chopped (reserve the peels, remove as much white pith as possible, and slice into thin strips)

1 cup (235 ml) Demerara Sugar Simple Syrup (see page 154)

2–4 cups (475–940 ml) yuzu vinegar

TIME: 48 HOURS. Combine the chopped tangerine segments and the sliced tangerine peels with the Demerara Simple Syrup in a nonreactive bowl, and stir to combine. Cover the bowl tightly and let the mixture sit for 24 hours, stirring several times to encourage fermentation and flavor development. Then add enough yuzu vinegar to cover the fruit mixture, and let it steep for another 24 hours. Finally, muddle the mixture a bit with a wooden spoon to release as much juice as possible from the tangerine segments, and strain the shrub into sterilized bottles or jars. Use immediately— or, if you have time, age in the fridge for a month shaking daily. It's wonderful with rum, vodka, and whiskey cocktails.

CHANCES IN THE FOG COCKTAIL

FEEL LIKE YOU'VE BEEN GROPING *your way through the day? We've all been there. Reward yourself for making it to quitting time with a Chances in the Fog Cocktail. London-style dry gin and fizzy seltzer water set off my savory, tangy Heirloom Tomato, Pear, and Sage Shrub to great effect—and a nip of aromatic bitters can help relax uneasy bellies. And speaking of the ameliorating effects of this cocktail, it's worth noting that sage may calm disorders of the upper respiratory system, such as asthma, while the lycopene in tomatoes may help prevent certain cancers and neurodegenerative diseases. And fiber-rich pears, it seemed, were prized for their anti-nausea qualities in ancient Greece. Just another good reason to take your Chances in the Fog.*

2 ounces (60 ml) London dry gin

1 ounce (30 ml) Heirloom Tomato, Pear, and Sage Shrub (see page 52)

½ ounce (15 ml) seltzer water

3 dashes aromatic bitters (such as my Cocktail Whisperer's Raw Honey Aromatic Bitters: see page 62)

Fill a cocktail glass three-quarters full with ice. Add the gin and the Heirloom Tomato, Pear, and Sage Shrub. Use a long cocktail spoon to stir the mixture for about 30 strokes. Use your Hawthorne strainer to strain the mixture into a coupe glass. Top with the aromatic bitters.

SARATOGA RACE DAY COCKTAIL

THANKS TO ITS FAMOUS *horse-racing track and its healing mineral springs, Saratoga Springs in upstate New York has had a reputation for being a playground for the rich and famous since the nineteenth century. During the six weeks that span the end of July and the beginning of September, the town's population mushrooms by as much as six figures, and visiting race- and partygoers have only one thing on their agenda: pleasure. What's more delightfully indulgent than starting your day with a breakfast cocktail? I envision the Saratoga Race Day Cocktail as the kickoff to a long, lazy day of leisure. Make a batch of them at your next weekend brunch, and serve them alongside eggs Benedict with thick slices of smoked bacon.*

3 ounces (90 ml) very smoky Scotch whisky, such as Lagavulin

3 ounces (90 ml) Grilled Tangerine Shrub (see page 53)

1 ounce (30 ml) champagne or dry sparkling wine

2–4 drops grapefruit bitters

Fill a Boston shaker three-quarters full with ice. Add the Scotch whisky and the Grilled Tangerine Shrub, and shake hard for 10 seconds. Place one cube of ice in an old-fashioned glass, and pour the mixture over it. Top with the champagne or sparkling wine, dot with the bitters, and serve.

Cocktail bitters, as we know them today, have been around since the nineteenth century, but bitters have been around for far longer than that. The tradition of combining botanicals like flower, bark, root, and spice essences and steeping them in alcohol stretches back at least to the ancient Egyptians. Recent studies have shown that they preserved precious medicinal herbs in wine to keep them from spoiling—just as European apothecaries would have done many centuries later. For both the ancient Egyptians and the early apothecaries, bitters were far more than tasty flavorings that could add zing to beverages: They were medicinal tonics that could heal a whole truckload of maladies, including digestive disorders, circulatory issues, nausea, loss of appetite, fever, and even coughs and colds.

Today, we know that lots of these claims aren't backed up by scientific proof. But close cousins of medicinal bitters are still on the market, such as Bach Flower remedies, which consist of flower essences mixed in a solution of water and brandy. These "remedies," which are meant to relieve symptoms of both physical and psychological distress, are placed by the drop under your tongue, or can be dripped onto a sugar cube and added to a glass of soda water. That's a technique that bears close resemblance to my favorite cure for hiccups: Just sprinkle a slice of lemon with sugar, dot it with bitters, and get the hiccupper to chomp down on it. It really works!

Bitters, essentially, are a boozy kind of tea—except botanicals are used in place of teabags, and are submerged in alcohol instead of water. After this "tea" has steeped for a while, it's strained or clarified before it's stored and consumed. That's a method that's been used in scores of countries worldwide—especially European countries—for centuries. Take, for example, the German digestive bitters called Underberg. Made from a top-secret recipe, they were (and are!) used to counteract the aches and pains brought on by a hangover or a heavy meal. (In fact, Underberg's slogan reads, "After a good meal.") In Italy, overindulgers turn to Fernet Branca, a popular digestif, for relief: it's a bitter *amaro* liqueur comprised of botanicals like rhubarb, chamomile, saffron, and cardamom. And American producers are on board with bitters, too: For instance, Vermont herbalists and beekeepers, originally from Caledonia in Scotland, prepare bitters that are made with distilled alcohol, raw honey, and elderberry liqueur. The result? A potent tonic that can be added to cool water—or even to locally distilled corn whiskey.

And they're not alone. These days, more and more American craft producers are making bitters—and that means a wide variety of flavors are available on the market. There's plenty to experiment with when you can get your hands on wildly inventive, flavored bitters that bear names like Curry, Sarsaparilla, Smoke Gets in your Bitters, West Indian Orange, Thai, Celery, Rhubarb, Black Walnut, Mint, Maple, and Coriander, to name only a very few. Yes sir, bitters sure have changed since the ancient Egyptians were preserving healing botanical essences in clay pots. Today, cocktail bitters truly are to mixologists what seasonings are to a chef. With their zippy jolts of flavor, all it takes is a drop or two to transform a ho-hum cocktail into a work of mixological art. (The same goes for shrubs.) And craft cocktails are all about working these new-yet-old types of concentrated flavors—sweet, sour, tangy, bitter—into fresh combinations.

That said, if you're feeling adventurous, you don't even have to buy bitters: You can make your own at home. And it's incredibly easy: Just check out my Cocktail Whisperer's Raw Honey Aromatic Bitters recipe on page 62. All you do is mix, steep, strain, and bottle—then use in any recipe that calls for bitters. And thanks to alcohol's preservative powers, they'll last practically forever. Try them in my Purgatorial Brandy Fizz—a cocktail that's sure to bring you back from the brink of hangover hell. (Bitters are renowned for their stomach-soothing abilities, remember?) It's a strengthening concoction of rye whiskey, apple brandy, and hard pear cider, finished off with home-made bitters, and it really does take the sting out of the morning, or after-noon, after. And speaking of day drinking, why not try a batch of the cocktail I call Reading the Paper at your next Sunday brunch? Grilled citrus juices are balanced by bitters, Drambuie, and *mezcal,* and the result is a pick-me-up that's a mixture of sweet, smoky, and tangy. And, believe it or not, bitters are fabulous in beer-based cocktails, so gird up your loins and make yourself a Just Down The Way from Paris, Texas. It's a tart, savory libation that fuses absinthe, a portion of my Grilled Tangerine Shrub, thyme leaves, and bitters with lager, and it's a great summertime aperitif.

And that's just a taster. Read on to find out how versatile bitters really are.

COCKTAIL WHISPERER'S RAW HONEY AROMATIC BITTERS

A LITTLE SPICY AND A LITTLE SWEET, *my own recipe for aromatic bitters is truly addictive—and it's unbelievably easy to make. In fact, the hardest part is doing the shopping. You'll find the raw honey, the Quassia and gentian extracts (and the spices, too) at your local health food shop, and then it's just a matter of buying sherry and grain alcohol, which preserves the mixture* ad infinitum. *Gentian extract, which is also found in the recipes for Angostura and Peychaud's Bitters, is a flower-based concentrate that has a venerable history of healing digestive ailments. Plus, it lends a deeper flavor and aroma to the bitters. Quassia extract is also great for maladies of the belly: It's used in* amaro-*type liqueurs, which are often enjoyed as digestifs.*

1 teaspoon gentian extract

2 tablespoons (30 g) Quassia extract

2 whole cinnamon sticks

1–2 (or more, to taste) dried birds-eye Thai chilies

$^1/_2$ ounce (15 g) freshly grated nutmeg

$^1/_2$ ounce (15 g) Chinese five-spice mix

$^1/_2$ ounce (15 g) star anise

$^1/_2$ ounce (15 g) fennel seeds

$^1/_2$ ounce (15 g) cardamom pods

375 ml (half of a 750 ml bottle) Spanish sherry (*oloroso* sherry works best because of its nutty, boldly assertive flavors)

1 750ml bottle of clear grain alcohol, such as Everclear

16 ounces (455 g) raw honey

Combine all the ingredients in a very large mixing bowl, and mix well. Then divide the mixture between two 1-quart (946 ml) Mason jars with tight rubber seals and sturdy glass tops. Store in the fridge or a cool, dark place, and shake vigorously twice daily for 1–2 months. Strain the mixture through cheesecloth to remove the spices, and then funnel into small, sterilized bottles. Use wherever bitters are called for in your food and drink.

Note: Use your homemade bitters in any recipe that calls for them, and don't limit yourself to cocktails: They add magic to lots of dishes, like a steaming, savory, creamless fish chowder.

SHIP OF FOOLS COCKTAIL

IT WAS LATER THAN I THOUGHT *when I woke up in New Orleans. How many different drinks had I consumed at that Tales of the Cocktail event? My throbbing head told me there were too many to count. I needed something to take the edge off. Fortunately, I knew I had a small bottle of Fernet Branca in my kit bag, along with samples of aromatic bitters from several different producers—and a bottle of aspirin. Whew. My* Ship of Fools Cocktail *is named for the suffering devils that forgot to pack a bottle of Fernet Branca or aromatic bitters before visiting the Big Easy in high summer. If you're one of them, find a sympathetic bartender to mix you up this restorative combo of Fernet, grilled-lemon juice, good-quality cane-sugar cola, finished off with a dash of bitters. Relief is just a few sips away.*

2 ounces (60 ml)
Fernet Branca

1 ounce (30 ml) grilled-lemon
juice (simply lightly sear
lemon rounds over an open
flame, then cool and juice)

lemon zest twists

3 ounces (90 ml)
cane-sugar cola

2-3 drops maple syrup
and rye whiskey
barrel-aged bitters

Fill a Boston shaker three-quarters full with ice. Add the Fernet Branca and the grilled-lemon juice to the shaker, and shake hard for 10 seconds. Rub a lemon zest twist around the rim of an old-fashioned glass, and add 2 large ice cubes; then add the Fernet Branca mixture, and top with the cola. Garnish with the lemon zest twist. Drip the bitters over the top for the win!

PURGATORIAL BRANDY FIZZ

NEXT TIME YOU FIND YOURSELF *in a purgatory of your own making after a little too much good food and wine, just relax: The Purgatorial Brandy Fizz is nothing short of a miracle worker. Here, spicy rye whiskey meets a measure of strong apple brandy and fizzy pear cider in a long, tall drink that's pure refreshment for flagging spirits. But don't be fooled, for the Fizz is in no way a sweet drink: After all, that's not what atonement for your sins is all about. However, the final flourish is probably the most medicinal: My aromatic bitters will sort out your stomach while the whiskey takes the edge off that headache. While the Purgatorial Fizz is a perfect remedy when you're feeling poorly, consider yourself forewarned that drinking more than four will send you to Hades and back.*

2 ounces (60 ml) rye whiskey

3/4 ounce (20 ml) 100-proof apple brandy

3/4 ounce (20 ml) hard pear cider (the carbonated kind)

5 drops Cocktail Whisperer's Raw Honey Aromatic Bitters (see page 62)

hand-cut ice cube

Fill a mixing glass three-quarters full with ice. Add the whiskey, apple brandy, and the pear cider, and stir 30 times (the mixture will fizz up: that's to be expected!). Pour the mixture over your hand-cut ice cubes into a Collins glass, and dot with the raw honey bitters to finish.

"READING THE PAPER"

PUT ON YOUR SLIPPERS, *curl up in your favorite easy chair, and get ready for a little R&R. I call this suave little number Reading the Paper because it's a wonderful accompaniment to that precious "me" time it's so hard to carve out for yourself. Grab the* Wall Street Journal, *that dog-eared copy of* Treasure Island, *the latest issue of* Time Out—*whatever your literary poison happens to be—and then kick back and relax with this beguiling cocktail by your side. It features mezcal, which tastes like a smoky tequila and marries well with honey-laden Drambuie: Then it enrobes the spirits in dressing-gowns of grilled-fruit juices. Intrigued? It gets better: Two varieties of bitters finish it off, adding balance and depth to the drink. Reading the Paper is wonderful alongside a late breakfast—like an Irish breakfast, complete with eggs, sausages, rashers of bacon, and fried bread—and a cup of strong black coffee. Day drinking? Why not?*

1 ounce (30 ml) Drambuie

2 ounces (60 ml) *mezcal*

1 ounce (30 ml) broiled grapefruit juice (sprinkle half a grapefruit with a teaspoon of Demerara sugar and broil until bubbly—then cool and juice)

1 ounce (30 ml) broiled orange juice (sprinkle half an orange with a teaspoon of Demerara sugar and broil until bubbly—then cool and juice)

2 drops black walnut bitters

2 drops plum bitters

Fill a Boston shaker three-quarters full with ice. Add all the ingredients except the bitters: cover, shake, and pour into an 8 ounce (235-ml) old-fashioned glass over a cube of hand-cut ice. Dot with two drops each of black walnut and plum bitters. Serve alongside a sigh of satisfaction.

A CHORUS OF VOICES COCKTAIL

THIS DELICIOUSLY TWISTED TAKE *on the gin and tonic restores nearly forgotten Old Tom gin to its former glory. Wildly popular in eighteenth-century London, Old Tom gin is now being rediscovered by craft distillers: It's sweeter than most contemporary gins, and that means it doesn't need a sugar-laden tonic water to balance it out. That's why the Chorus of Voices calls upon a variety of piquant flavors: a little rum, a dose of my Nectarine, Celery, and Black Pepper Shrubb, and a good dry tonic water—or even plain seltzer. What's the perfect finale to such a chorus? Two types of bitters, including grapefruit bitters, which add an astringent, assertive finish, plus the crunch of a pinch of* fleur de sel. *The finished product is so memorable that you'll be through with those boring old G&Ts for good.*

large cubes of hand-cut ice

2 ounces (60 ml) Old Tom-style gin

1/2 ounce (15 ml) *Rhum Agricole*

1 ounce (30 ml) Nectarine, Celery, and Black Pepper Shrubb (see page 33)

1 ounce (30 ml) cane-sugar based tonic water (or seltzer, for a drier finish)

2 dashes West Indian orange bitters

2 dashes grapefruit bitters

pinch of *fleur de sel*

grapefruit zest twist

Add two cubes of hand-cut ice to a large goblet. Add the gin, the *Rhum Agricole,* and the Nectarine, Celery, and Black Pepper Shrubb. Top with the tonic water, then the bitters. Finish with the *fleur de sel,* and garnish with a long grapefruit zest twist—then wait for your guests to demand an encore.

THE JIMMY GILLESPIE FIZZ

IT'S EASY TO SHOWCASE THE *depth of flavor inherent in bitters. The key? Simplicity. When you add a dash of your favorite bitters to a glass of spirits mixed with seltzer water, you'll find that all the heavy lifting has been done for you. Take, for example, the Jimmy Gillespie Fizz, named after a dear friend of mine from Swan's Island, Maine. He was one-of-a-kind: an old codger from another generation. Jimmy loved his Scotch, and he inducted me into the pleasures of drinking fine, single-malt Scotch whisky with as few embellishments as possible: except, perhaps, a tiny bit of his brackish-tasting well water alongside the whisky, or maybe a few dashes of bitters. Bitters, he claimed, healed the belly, although I suspect he was more partial to their astringent taste—and their alcohol content.*

That was Jimmy for you.

2 ounces (60 ml) Scotch whisky

6 shakes of aromatic bitters

small splash of seltzer water

lemon zest twist

Add the Scotch whiskey to a cocktail glass. Top with a few shakes of the aromatic bitters, and then finish with a dribble of seltzer and a lemon zest twist. Nothing more to do except lift a glass to Jimmy.

WHAT I'M ABOUT TO TELL *you will change your life. Here it comes: bitters are marvelous in beer. And the Just Down The Way From Paris, Texas, is living proof. There's nothing complicated about it, but it does feature a couple of clever twists. The first is a little absinthe; the second, a portion of my Grilled Tangerine Shrub. When you combine the two with a good lager and a few drops of my homemade bitters, you get a cocktail that's guaranteed to quench your thirst, even in the face of desert-level temperatures. A few leaves of fresh thyme crown the savory Just Down The Way: Don't omit them, since they're such a good match for the shrub. And if you're in the market for a good absinthe, try French-made Tenneyson Absinthe Royale—it's one of my favorites.*

**2 ounces (60 ml)
Grilled Tangerine Shrub
(see page 53)**

**8 ounces (235 ml)
lager beer**

**1/2 ounce (15 ml) Tenneyson
Absinthe Royale (France)**

**4 drops Cocktail Whisperer's
Raw Honey Aromatic Bitters
(see page 62)**

thyme leaves, for garnish

Add the Grilled Tangerine Shrub to a beer glass. Top with the beer and mix with a swizzle stick (I use a Belgian triple-style ale with a bit more alcohol). Pour the Absinthe over the top. Finish with 4 drops of the homemade cocktail bitters for good health and garnish with a sprig of fresh thyme.

WE'VE ESTABLISHED THAT, *having discovered the pleasures of beer cocktails, your life has been changed irrevocably. So far, so good. Now, I hope you've been enjoying them before meals, because beer cocktails make fabulous—and fabulously effective—aperitifs. Consider yourself introduced, then, to the assertive, interrogative, straight-talking cocktail that is the I Beg Your Pardon, Sir? Here, Thai basil jabs your palate in the ribs with its peppery, spicy notes before chile-laden Thai bitters take over the job, adding an extra whack of heat and flavor. (There are plenty of good-quality Thai bitters on the market. Or, you can make your own by whipping up a batch of my Cocktail Whisperer's Raw Honey Aromatic Bitters—see page 62—and tripling the amount of chiles.) Refreshing and full of joie de vivre, this is what you want pre-barbeque on a hot summer's day.*

2 ounces (60 ml) Rhum Agricole

4 ounces (120 ml) oak barrel-aged Belgian ale, such as Rodenbach Ale

3 drops Thai bitters

sprig of Thai basil, slapped

Add the Rhum Agricole to a goblet or large Burgundy wine glass. Top with the ale, and dot the bitters over the top of the drink. Place the sprig of Thai basil in the palm of your hand and slap it with your other hand, releasing its essential oils. Float the slapped basil in the cocktail, and serve immediately.

THE CLASP KNIFE COCKTAIL

BACK IN THE DAY, A SEAMAN *would have used his clasp knife to repair the ship's rigging and cordage—which meant he'd have to climb high up onto the yardarms above the roiling sea. This strong, tart cocktail takes its name from that essential tool. And beware: like its namesake, it's got a surprisingly sharp edge. Be sure to make it with Belgian-style "sour" ale, not traditional ale. Sour ale is a beer with an acidic taste that's made by introducing various yeasts into the brewing process, unlike "regular" ale, which is brewed in a sterile environment. Its flavor is a great partner for my Ginger-Lime Shrubb, and together they balance the potency of* Rhum Agricole *and Pineau des Charentes (a sweet, fortified wine). Landlubbers who indulge in too many of these little firecrackers may need to be dosed with Angostura bitters the next morning to make the pain go away.*

2 ounces (60 ml) Pineau des Charentes

2 ounces (60 ml) 100-proof *Rhum Agricole*

2 ounces (60 ml) Ginger-Lime Shrubb (see page 20)

1 ounce (30 ml) Belgian-style "sour" ale

2 dashes lime bitters (for preventing scurvy, of course)

Add the Pineau and the *Rhum Agricole* to a beer goblet. Add the Lime Ginger Shrubb and mix well (you can use ice, if you like, although ice wouldn't have been available in the great age of sail). Pour the sour ale over the mixture, and finish with the lime bitters.

TWISTED CACHAÇA SOUR

BITTERS AREN'T FOR SAVORY *cocktails only. They've long been key features of tropical libations, like the famous Peruvian Pisco Sour. In this twisted version of that classic, I've replaced the Pisco with Cachaça, a kind of sugarcane–based, barrel-aged, distilled spirit that's the very soul of Brazil. Drinking Cachaça-laden cocktails can be very dangerous in hot weather: They go down with a treacherous smoothness until, all of a sudden, they whack you in the side of the head—so don't indulge in more than two at the very most. After you smash your ice (use a Lewis bag, which is made of canvas: It'll help wick the moisture away from the smashed ice), there's nothing difficult about making this Twisted Pisco: You just mix, shake, and dot with flavor-enhancing grapefruit bitters.*

3 ounces (90 ml) Cachaça

1/2 ounce (15 ml) green chartreuse

1 ounce (30 ml) Ginger-Lime Shrub (see page 20)

1/2 ounce (15 ml) freshly squeezed lime juice

1 egg white

smashed ice

3 drops grapefruit bitters

Mix the Cachaça and chartreuse with the Ginger-Lime Shrub. Add the fresh lime juice, the Basic Simple Syrup, and the egg white to your Boston Shaker, and then add enough bar ice to fill to shaker three-quarters full. Cap and shake hard for 15 seconds. Put a fistful of smashed ice into a coupe glass, and pour the mixture over. Dot grapefruit bitters directly on top of the egg white foam, and serve.

It takes very little research to realize that the essential components in drinks haven't changed too much over the centuries. Bitters are still made by steeping flower essences, roots, and spices in liquor. Acerbic, botanical-rich digestifs like Campari or Underberg still improve digestion after a sumptuous meal. And shrubs are still simple, flavorful combinations of fruit, sugar, and vinegar—just like they were centuries ago.

Don't believe me? Walk into a local rum shop in any one of the Caribbean islands, and you'll see dozens of containers of shrubs and handcrafted rums in plain bottles. You might also see dozens of unmarked bottles, holding important elixirs and tonics, lining the -walls. These rum tonics are medicinal elixirs, filled with all sorts of roots, herbs, and spices. Each rum-based mixture is imbued with a specific healing power, and their ingredients have been revered as powerful health aids throughout the centuries. (Some of those glass bottles might even contain more potent ingredients, like pickled snakes and sea creatures. Don't ask too many questions: Just know that each elixir performs a specific—and vital—healing function. Then take your rum and leave.)

For all the technological advances the last century has seen, the essential ingredients in great cocktails haven't changed much since seventeenth-century buccaneers braved the seas in the hopes of looting lucrative merchant ships. That's where this chapter on classic shrub- and bitter-related recipes comes in. It's full of my Cocktail Whisperer's take on tried-and-true recipes that have their roots in centuries past. Just as they would have done in days of yore, aromatic bitters feature heavily in this chapter. (If you haven't made my Raw Honey Aromatic Bitters yet, now's the time to do it! Check out page 62.) They add a piquancy to one of my favorite recipes: a simple infusion of hot chili peppers in vinegar and sherry wine that's a delicious addition to both cuisine and craft cocktails—including my grown-up version of the tequila sunrise.

Let's not forget shrubs, though. The shrub recipes in this chapter are based on flavors that George Washington himself would have recognized. My Grilled Peach and Thai Basil shrub preserves the essence of farm-fresh peaches for months. And my Spiced Cherry Shrub is another time-honored concoction: Cherries have been cultivated for at least two millennia (and who can forget the famous cherry-tree anecdote extolling the honesty of a young George?).

And lots of the recipes in this chapter showcase classic liquors with august pedigrees, like handmade Caribbean Rhum Agricole and top-quality American bourbon. Then there's vermouth, which can boast quite a history. Its name is derived from the French pronunciation of the German word *Wermut*, meaning "wormwood." (Wormwood, by the way, isn't really "wood:" it's actually a leafy, herbaceous plant.) We often associate wormwood with absinthe, but back in the day it was a traditional ingredient in vermouth as well, and has been thought to be beneficial to sore bellies for millennia. Wormwood is effective against intestinal worms and head lice! So now you know what to do with your vermouth that has gone sour!

Enough talking. Let's start mixing! I hope you've got my Sherry Pepper Infusion steeping away in the fridge, because it's crucial to my Shall We Talk Business, Madam? Cocktail. It's a near neighbor to the traditional Scotch sour, in which fresh lemon juice, simple syrup, and Scotch whisky reign—but a couple drops of bitters and a couple more of the spicy Sherry Pepper Infusion add complexity and character to it. Make that Grilled Peach and Thai Basil Shrubb, and then use it in my Mendham Cocktail, where it mingles with bourbon, rum, a pinch of *fleur de sel,* and the twenty-first century addition of Moroccan bitters. And research shows that cherries may

have anti-inflammatory and pain-reducing properties, so use my Spiced Cherry Shrub with impunity in the Old Homesteader's Surfeit, where the sweet-tart shrub is a toothsome match for bourbon. (*Nota bene*: always make your own ice from bottled spring water, and hand-cut your own if you can. Or, invest in the silicone rubber ice trays that are widely available. Freshly made ice lets the flavors in your handcrafted cocktails sing.)

Get behind the bar, and start experimenting with the bitters and shrubs that have been delighting drinkers for centuries.

SHERRY PEPPER INFUSION

ON THE ISLAND OF BERMUDA, *a British protectorate that boasts a long history of shrub-making, residents preserve hot chili peppers with sherry and aromatic bitters for a table-to-glass condiment that's intensely hot and powerful. My Sherry Pepper Infusion is delicious in cool, savory cocktails like Bloody Marys, and it adds a piquant flourish to cooked fish dishes when served tableside. You can make this with a darker, older variety of sherry with a more robust mouthfeel, like* oloroso *or* Pedro Ximénez, *but it'll take several months (or even up to a year) to mature—whereas this version, made with crisp, aromatic, refreshing* fino *sherry, takes only a month. Word to the wise: Wear gloves when you chop insanely hot bird's eye chilies. Otherwise, their essential oils will cling to your skin, even after you wash your hands.*

6 ounces (175 ml) *fino*
(very dry) sherry

**6 ounces (175 ml)
sherry vinegar**

**2 tablespoons (30 g)
chopped fresh Thai bird's eye
chili peppers**

**2 teaspoons
Angostura bitters**

Combine all ingredients in a sterilized bottle or jar, then cap and store in a cool, dry place, or the refrigerator, for a month or more before using. Then, use (sparingly!) in dishes or drinks that are served cool, like jellied *madrilène* soup, or in a batch of Bloody Marys.

SHALL WE TALK OF BUSINESS, MADAM?

THE MADAM IN QUESTION *is Mrs. McRankine, a venerable Scottish widow with a formidable amount of spice in her language in Robert Louis Stevenson's unfinished novel,* St. Ives. *This cocktail is named for her, and, like Mrs. McRankine herself, it certainly speaks its mind. A couple drops of my Sherry Pepper Infusion add a hot, bitter-laden zing to smoky Scotch whisky—then, equal measures of a raw honey–based simple syrup and fresh lemon juice add a little sweetness and a burst of acidity. If you like whisky sours, you'll love this spiced-up kissing cousin of the classic drink. Serve yourself a Shall We Talk Of Business, Madam? before dinner along with a handful of sea-salted, roasted almonds: It slices right through the nuts' salty, oily crunch.*

2 ounces (60 ml) Scotch whisky

2 drops Sherry Pepper Infusion (see page 80)

1 ounce (30 ml) Raw Honey Simple Syrup (see page 152)

1 ounce (30 ml) freshly squeezed lemon juice

2 drops Cocktail Whisperer's Raw Honey Aromatic Bitters (see page 62)

Fill a Boston shaker three-quarters full with ice. Add the whisky, the Sherry Pepper Infusion, the Raw Honey Simple Syrup, and the lemon juice, and then cap and shake vigorously for 10 seconds. Strain the mixture into a rocks glass over a single cube of hand-cut ice. Drip the bitters over the top, and serve.

THE GRENADIER COCKTAIL

NEED TO ADD A LITTLE VITAMIN C *to your diet? The Grenadier Cocktail is just what the doctor ordered, and it's based on a combination that's been around since time immemorial. Like the classic Tequila Sunrise cocktail, it combines tequila, citrus juice and grenadine—but it's not your everyday mix of budget tequila, concentrated orange juice, and bottled, artificially colored grenadine syrup. Reposado tequila, three types of freshly squeezed citrus juice, and homemade grenadine mean serious mixological business is happening here. And a final flourish of homemade bitters turns the Grenadier into a truly elegant aperitif. Relax: Making your own grenadine is really easy, and it's so much better than the stuff you get from a bottle or a can.*

2 ounces (60 ml) **reposado** tequila

¼ ounce (7 ml) Homemade Grenadine (see page 154)

¼ ounce (7 ml) each freshly squeezed lemon, lime, and orange juices

3 drops Cocktail Whisperer's Raw Honey Aromatic Bitters (see page 62)

Add all the ingredients except the bitters to a Boston shaker. Top the ingredients with enough ice to fill the shaker three-quarters full. Cover and shake hard for 15 seconds. Strain the mixture into a coupe glass and dot the bitters over the top.

GRILLED PEACH AND THAI BASIL SHRUB

WHENEVER I FIND MYSELF WITH *less-than-perfect-looking produce on hand, I head straight to the grill. Grilling is a great way to harness the flavors of slightly overripe fruits and vegetables. It transforms their flavor profiles by bringing out their natural sugars. And grilled produce is lovely when it's turned into a shrub. Think of caramelized peaches and peppery basil, which are a great match for one another. You could easily turn them into a summery salad, drizzled with a balsamic reduction—but I like to turn them into a shrub so that I can enjoy their bright flavors for months after peaches are out of season. Try to let this shrub age for a full month before you use it, since it definitely improves with age. (And as always, I implore you to use fresh ingredients—always. If a recipe calls for produce that's out of season, replace it with a similar seasonal ingredient, and change the recipe accordingly. Never ever use the canned or frozen variety if you can help it.)*

2-3 pounds (1-1.5 kg) peaches, quartered, then grilled over hardwood charcoal until lightly charred (or roasted for 30 minutes at 400°F [200°C, or gas mark 6] until lightly browned), then cooled and chopped

1 cup (200 g) Demerara sugar

1-2 pinches of *fleur de sel*

1 cup (235 ml) sherry vinegar

1 cup (24 g) Thai basil, leaves only

Place the cooked peaches in a nonreactive bowl, then cover with the Demerara sugar and sea salt. Stir well to combine, then cover tightly and place the bowl in the fridge or a cool, dark place, stirring several times daily for about 2 days. Place a sieve over another nonreactive bowl, and then transfer the mixture to a nonreactive sieve. Use a wooden spoon to press the slightly fermented peach solids and liquids through the sieve. Discard the fruit pulp. Add the vinegar and the Thai basil; stir again, then let the mixture sit for a few hours. Funnel the shrub into sterilized bottles or jars, then store in the fridge for a month, shaking the bottle or jar a couple times daily. (Patience is a necessary ingredient in this shrub!) It's delicious in my Mendham Cocktail.

MENDHAM COCKTAIL

SOME OF THE SWEETEST PEACHES *I've ever slurped are grown in and around Mendham, a rural New Jersey town, located about an hour north-by-northwest of New York City. Historically, Mendham was the location of the winter encampment for George Washington's Continental Army—and I'll bet my wages that those Mendham peaches were just as delicious two and a half centuries ago as they are today. This cocktail puts my Grilled Peach and Thai Basil Shrubb in the driver's seat, alongside a good bourbon like Four Roses and soupcon of* Rhum Agricole—*its sweetly perfumed flavor profile makes for a haunting, memorable finish. A zap of fizzy water and a few drops of spicy Moroccan-style cocktail bitters—a twenty-first century emendation—and the job's done. The next step? Get ready to make a second round.*

2 ounces (60 ml) small-batch bourbon whiskey, such as Four Roses

¹/₂ ounce (15 ml) *Rhum Agricole*

2 ounces (60 ml) Grilled Peach and Thai Basil Shrubb (see page 84)

splash of fizzy water

Moroccan-style bitters

pinch of *fleur de sel*

Fill a Collins glass with hand-cut ice. Pour the bourbon, the *Rhum Agricole*, and the shrub over it. Add the fizzy water, and stir gently with a long cocktail spoon. Dash the Moroccan bitters over the top of the cocktail, followed by the *fleur de sel*. Fin!

SCRIVENER'S CAMP

FEATURING A FINAL FLOURISH *of luscious, dark chocolate bitters, this bracing cocktail is named for the men (and they usually were men) who, unlike many of their peers, could read and write. These gentlemen could be hired to perform secretarial duties for the population at large—most of whom were illiterate. Beware: After a couple rounds of Scrivener's Camps, you may well need a scrivener to sign your name in your stead. That's because three types of liquor work their potent magic in this cocktail: bourbon, absinthe, and, not least, vermouth, which was originally manufactured as a hair tonic and scalp invigorator because of the exotic herbs, flower essences, and spices contained in each bottle. (My thoughts? Avoid this. Stick to applying vermouth to your mouth only.) Here, a wash of absinthe gives the bitters a chance to act as a foil against the sweetness of the bourbon and vermouth in this historically inspired cocktail.*

2 ounces (60 ml) bourbon, such as Four Roses

1/2 ounce (15 ml) sweet vermouth, such as Carpano Antica

1 ounce (30 ml) freshly squeezed grapefruit juice

1/2 ounce (15 ml) absinthe

several drops of chocolate bitters

Easy Home-Cured Cocktail Cherries (see page 154), for garnish

Fill a cocktail mixing glass half full with ice. Add the bourbon, the vermouth, and the grapefruit juice, and stir about 20 times to combine. Then pour the absinthe into a coupe glass: You can either drink it immediately and leave its residue in the glass as a glass wash, or you can leave the full portion of absinthe in the glass (I prefer the latter). Strain the bourbon mixture over the absinthe into the coupe glass; dot the top of the cocktail with the chocolate bitters, and garnish with an Easy Home-Cured Cocktail Cherry.

SPICED CHERRY SHRUB

WITH THEIR TART, CRIMSON FLESH *and their finger-staining juices, cherries have been the very embodiment of summertime since time immemorial. Of course, the tragedy is that their growing season is so short, comprising just a few weeks around mid-June or mid-July. It's a shame that we can't eat local cherries all year round—but we sure can turn them into luscious shrubs. This Spiced Cherry Shrub combines the toothsome fruits with lemon zest, cinnamon, and a punch of Chinese five-spice powder, and the result is a fragrant liquid that's an excellent complement to cocktails. And an added bonus is the spice-laden cherry pulp that you'll have left over. Don't toss it out: it makes a fabulous condiment to both sweet and savory dishes.*

1 pound (455 g) dark red cherries, pitted and picked over for stems and stones (you don't want to break any teeth, do you?) and roughly chopped

1 cup (200 g) Demerara sugar

2 teaspoons Chinese five-spice powder

1 cinnamon stick

zest of 1 Meyer lemon (avoid the bitter white pith)

1 cup (235 ml) sweet balsamic vinegar

Place the cherries in a nonreactive bowl and cover with the sugar. Mix well to combine. Cover tightly, and let the mixture sit on your kitchen counter for 1–2 days. Then add the spices, the cinnamon, the lemon zest, and the vinegar, and mix to combine; let the fruit and vinegar mixture steep in the fridge for 1 week. Then place a nonreactive strainer over another nonreactive bowl, and transfer the fruit and vinegar mixture to it, using a wooden spoon to press as much of the fruit pulp and liquid through the strainer as possible. (Reserve the fruit pulp for cooking. Hide it from your enemies, who may long to filch these luscious cherries to spice up vanilla ice cream or a roast pork loin. It will happen, so guard against it.) Funnel the liquid into a sterilized bottle or jar, close tightly, and age in the fridge for 1 month. It's delicious in whiskey-based cocktails.

OLDE HOMESTEADER'S SURFEIT COCKTAIL

AFTER A SUCCESSFUL LATE-SUMMER *harvest, some lucky farmers might have had more cherries than they knew what to do with. That's where shrub-making would have come in: A farmer's wife would have "put up" plenty of a cherry-based shrub to preserve the essence of summery cherries for the long winter months ahead. My own sumptuous Spiced Cherry Shrub is great in cocktails. It practically demands attention from whiskey in all its forms. (Think bourbon, Scotch, or rye.) The Olde Homesteader's Surfeit—which calls for only a few simple ingredients—is the perfect early-autumn cocktail: Just toss together bourbon, my Spiced Cherry Shrub, and aromatic bitters—then zap the mixture with a little seltzer water, and sit back and sip. If you're too impatient to let your Spiced Cherry Shrub mature, mix up my instant version by combining cherry preserves with a little balsamic vinegar.*

2 ounces (60 ml) bourbon (or whiskey of your choice)

1 ounce (30 ml) Spiced Cherry Shrub (see page 89)—or, make your own quick shrub by mixing 1 tablespoon (15 g) cherry preserves with 1 tablespoon (15 ml) balsamic vinegar

1 ounce (30 ml) seltzer water

2-3 shakes of my Cocktail Whisperer's Raw Honey Aromatic Bitters (see page 62)

Fill a Boston shaker three-quarters full with ice, and pour the bourbon and the cherry shrub over it. Cap and shake hard. Strain the mixture into a coupe glass, and top with a splash of seltzer water. Finish with a couple drops of my Raw Honey Aromatic Bitters.

As the saying goes, there's nothing new under the sun. I'm not sure who came up with that one, but when it comes to cocktails, it's the truth, by George. Lots of the craft cocktails we enjoy in our favorite bars today have their roots firmly embedded in the past. And that's a very good thing. The recipes for classic cocktails have stood the test of time for a reason: They're just as delicious today as they were when they were invented years—even centuries—ago. And what's more, these traditional recipes can act as valuable templates, giving adventurous bartenders, both amateur and professional, plenty of room to experiment.

That's where bitters and shrubs come in. I've found that nearly any classic cocktail recipe can be made even more memorable through the well-placed application of some sort of creatively flavored cocktail bitters or homemade shrubs—or both. Take, for example, the esteemed mint julep, a mixture of bourbon, sugar, fresh mint leaves, and water. Now, let's deconstruct it a bit. What would happen, an inventive mixologist might ask her- or himself, if I replaced the mint with mint-flavored bitters? Or, even better, what if I were to use both? And what if I replaced the traditional bourbon with rye, or even dark rum? Alternatively, consider the champagne cocktail, which has been around for about a century. It involves a sugar cube topped with bitters and popped into a champagne flute, then drowned in cognac and champagne. What if, our theoretical mixologist might conjecture, I could add a portion of my homemade blackberry-fennel shrub to it—as well as a couple of key ingredients from the French 75, another champagne-based cocktail? I'd have created a brand-new drink. Suddenly, the possibilities presented by classic craft cocktails are endless—and it's incredibly exciting.

That said, when it comes to experimenting with the classics, I like to keep things simple. Most of the time, there's no need to go overboard with the number of ingredients you use. It's time-consuming, fiddly, and, more importantly, using a ton of ingredients doesn't necessarily mean you'll produce a better cocktail. So do what most of the recipes in this chapter do, and stick to that sweet spot of just four or five ingredients per cocktail. This way you won't spend a quarter of an hour preparing each drink when you've got a party full of thirsty guests waiting—even if it's a party of one. And, as always, stick to fresh ingredients in all your cocktails, and be sure to use handmade ice. After all, you're investing lots of time, patience, and skill into your carefully crafted drinks, so honor them by using the best-quality ingredients you can afford.

So, what's on the menu in this chapter? There are so many ways to twist up the classics that entire books could be written on the subject. And I'm delighted to pay homage to some of them here, since they're the drinks that made the cocktail business great back in the old days. Just like the original recipes, the cocktails here aren't showy or ostentatious. You'll find that no special effects are necessary—you won't be setting anything on fire—and the ingredients for each recipe are pretty minimal. Think of my Oblique Manhattan: Instead of the usual rye, vermouth, and bitters, it marries bourbon to a shot of my Spiced Cherry Shrub and ties the knot with a dash of absinthe and homemade bitters. Or, look to my Ginger-Lime Daiquiri for proof. Banish thoughts of those sugary frozen drinks you find at chain restaurants: This is a riff on the real thing, a threesome of rum, fresh lime juice, and a little simple syrup. But this twisted version calls for a dose of my Ginger-Lime Shrub, which I'm sure you have chilling in the fridge or the cellar by now, and the result is limey, tangy heaven. For a new take on a

BASEMENT BITTERS
GENUINE BARREL AGED

BITTER FROST

AROMATIC
BITTERS FROM
RYE SPIRIT

125ML   4.2 FL.OZ.

46 % A.B.V.

venerable English libation that's sure to satisfy a crowd, try my English Afternoon Punch, which calls for two hefty cups of my Blood Orange Shrub, citrus juices, and Scotch—plus a bottle of sweet-yet-mysteriously-smoky Drambuie. Serve it Prohibition-style: that is, in a vintage china teapot, to be poured out and served by the teacupful.

And that's just a glimpse of what's to come. Read on and discover more ways to reinvent classic cocktails with top-quality bitters and homemade shrubs.

AN OBLIQUE MANHATTAN

THE MANHATTAN IS PROBABLY *the preeminent classic American cocktail: It's been around since at least the late nineteenth century. Every bartender knows how to make one, and since it can sustain so many variations, its recipe is a template that creative mixologists love to tinker with. And I'm one of them. While the standard version is usually made with whiskey, sweet vermouth, and bitters, my Oblique Manhattan combines bourbon, a dose of my delectable Spiced Cherry Shrub, and a whisper of absinthe. (According to some sources, very early versions of the Manhattan originally included absinthe, so I like to think that my variation on the theme tips its hat to a proto-Manhattan now lost amongst the mists of time.) Bitters and an orange zest twist are a traditionally inspired finish to my twisted Manhattan. It's the pre-dinner drink: Serve it with just about any kind of* hors d'oeuvre—*or be a purist, and enjoy it on its own.*

2 ounces (60 ml) good-quality bourbon, such as Four Roses Yellow Label

¼ teaspoon absinthe

1 ounce (30 ml) Spiced Cherry Shrub (see page 89)

1 ounce (30 ml) vermouth, such as Carpano Antica

2–4 drops aromatic bitters

orange zest twist

Fill a cocktail mixing glass three-quarters full with ice. Add all the liquid ingredients except the bitters, and stir slowly about 30 times. (Never, ever shake a Manhattan! Bad things will happen.) Strain, using a Hawthorne strainer, into a short rocks glass and garnish with the orange zest twist. Top with 2–4 drops of aromatic bitters.

GINGER-LIME RUM DAIQUIRI

HAVE YOU EVER HAD A REAL DAIQUIRI? *I don't mean that syrupy, pseudo-fruity red stuff topped with rubbishy rum. The classic daiquiri, which has been around since the early twentieth century, has nothing to do with the artificially colored variety that comes in bottles or cans. I'm talking about the real thing: a trinity of handcrafted white rum, freshly squeezed lime juice, and a little simple syrup. If this doesn't sound familiar already, consider yourself introduced. But instead of starting you off with the traditional recipe, I'm going to throw you into the deep end with my twisted version of the rum daiquiri. Here, a mere ounce (30 ml) of my Ginger-Lime Shrubb adds extra tartness and pep to the rum-lime-sugar triumvirate. The result is a straight-up, ginger-laced cocktail that's as bracing as a margarita—and as refreshing on a warm day.*

2 ounces (60 ml) *Rhum Agricole*

1 ounce (30 ml) Ginger-Lime Shrubb (see page 20)

³/₄ ounce (20 ml) freshly squeezed lime juice

¹/₂ ounce (15 ml) Basic Simple Syrup (see page 152)

lime wheel, for garnish

Fill a Boston shaker three-quarters full with ice. Add all the liquid ingredients to the shaker, and shake hard for about 15 seconds. Strain into a martini glass, garnish with a lime wheel, and serve.

MINT JULEP CURIOSITY

WHEN I SAY "JULEP," *what's the first thing that pops into your mind? I bet it's "mint." And with good reason: the mint julep is centuries old, and dates back at least to the eighteenth century. But juleps didn't always involve mint: In fact, the term "julep" referred to a curative mixture of water, sugar, and spirits that could be used as a vehicle for medicines, or for steeping herbs in. My Mint Julep Curiosity may not be exactly medicinal, but it sure is an attitude adjuster, and it's a quirky take on the classic M.J. Sure, it includes fresh mint, rye whiskey, and simple syrup, but it's spiked with root tea liqueur, a quick and easy orange shrub, bittersweet chocolate syrup (it works, trust me!) and mint bitters. I'm sure my Southern friends rue the day that chocolate bitters made their way into a mint julep, but—unless you're a staunch purist—fear not: This Curiosity is intriguing, refreshing, and delicious.*

5–6 fresh mint leaves

4 drops mint bitters

1/2 ounce (15 ml) Basic Simple Syrup (see page 152)

2 ounces (60 ml) rye whiskey

1/2 ounce (15 ml) organic root tea liqueur

1/4 ounce (7 ml) bittersweet chocolate syrup

1 ounce (30 ml) Instant Orange Shrub (simply combine 1 tablespoon (15 g) orange marmalade with 1 tablespoon (15 ml) cider vinegar)

crushed ice

Place the mint in your grandpappy's sterling silver julep cup. Muddle the mint with 2 drops of the mint bitters, the Basic Simple Syrup, and a bit of the crushed ice. Then add the rye whiskey, the root tea liqueur, the chocolate syrup, and the orange shrub. Add more ice (and a little more rye, if you like) and mix until the julep cup is nicely frosted, inside and out. Finish with 2 more drops of the mint bitters, and then serve. Kentucky Derby optional.

BLACKBERRY-FENNEL SHRUB

Made from produce that would have grown wild in America's early days, this very special classic shrub is delicious during the summer, when plump blackberries are at their ripest. The boldly flavored, fragile fruits favor fennel, which has a lightly licoricey scent and taste—and grilling fennel really brings out that subtle aniseed flavor. And both fennel and blackberries can boast health-boosting properties: The former is great for digestion, while the latter is packed with vitamins C and K. A bonus: this shrub is relatively quick to make and is ready to use in just two weeks, so you won't have to wait long to enjoy it.

1 cup (455 g) fresh
blackberries, halved

1 cup (200 g)
Demerara sugar

1 cup (235 ml)
sherry vinegar

1 tablespoon (15 g) grilled
fennel, (bulb only, of course,
no fronds), finely chopped

1 tablespoon (15 g)
pink peppercorns

TIME: 2 WEEKS. Place the blackberries in a nonreactive bowl, and add the sugar. Mash the fruit and sugar together, then stir well and cover tightly. Leave to sit for 24 hours at room temperature. Then add the vinegar, fennel, and pink peppercorns. Stir well, cover tightly, and leave the mixture either in the fridge or at cellar temperature for 3–4 days. Then, place a nonreactive strainer over another nonreactive bowl and transfer the mixture to the strainer. Press down on the fruit-vinegar mixture with the back of a wooden spoon to release as much liquid from the blackberries as possible. Discard the fruit pulp. Funnel the liquid into a sterilized bottle or jar. Store in the refrigerator for another week or two, shaking the jar daily to combine the flavors and mellow the vinegar.

IT'S HARD TO IMPROVE UPON *the classic French 75—but it's not impossible. Named for the 75-millimeter M1897, a French gun used in the First World War, because of its powerful kick, the traditional French 75 involves gin, simple syrup, lemon juice, and champagne. My twisted version keeps the kick, but riffs on the original by skipping the lemon juice, and adding the necessary acidity by bolstering the gin-champagne combination with a portion of my delectable, summery Blackberry-Fennel Shrub. And it grafts on a notable characteristic of the good old-fashioned champagne cocktail: a bitters-laden sugar cube. As We Approached Saint-Denis tips its hat to the bushes full of sumptuous fruit that line the roadways near the French town of the same name. Serve a round of these elegant cocktails to a few thirsty birds, right before a leisurely warm-weather lunch.*

brown sugar cube

2 drops Cocktail Whisperer's Raw Honey Aromatic Bitters (see page 62)

1 ounce (30 ml) gin

1 ounce (30 ml) Blackberry-Fennel Shrub

2 ounces (60 ml) champagne

1 plump blackberry, for garnish

sprig of mint

Place the brown sugar cube into a champagne flute. Moisten with a few drops of my Raw Honey Aromatic Bitters. Then add the gin, the blackberry-fennel shrub, and top with some darned good champagne. Garnish with a single blackberry and a sprig of mint. Avoid having more than four of these little darlings at one go. You'll thank me later.

BITTER, TWISTED SIDECAR

WE ALL KNOW AND LOVE THE SIDECAR, *a tart threesome of brandy, Cointreau, and freshly squeezed lemon juice. It's a timeless classic, and it's been around since the early twentieth century, although incarnations of tart cocktails featuring brandy go back at least to the previous century. Named for the motorcycle attachment (although the reasons for this are nothing if not obscure), the sidecar is a staple of twenty-first century cocktail bars everywhere. I like to add a few variations to the theme, though. Here, a whisper of absinthe coats the glass; my Italian Blood Orange and Charred Rosemary Shrub replaces the traditional Cointreau; and a couple of drops of my homemade bitters round things off nicely. And don't forget to frost the rim of the glass. Pour a little freshly squeezed lemon juice into a saucer; dunk the rim in the juice; and then dunk it into a saucer of sugar that's been mixed with the tiniest pinch of cayenne pepper.*

few drops Tenneyson Absinthe Royale

2 ounces (60 ml) cognac

1 ounce (30 ml) Italian Blood Orange and Charred Rosemary Shrub (see page 40)

¼ ounce (7 ml) freshly squeezed lemon juice, strained

2 drops Cocktail Whisperer's Raw Honey Aromatic Bitters (see page 62)

Swirl a few drops of the absinthe around a coupe glass, then pour the absinthe out (into your mouth: no wasting good liquor!) Set aside. Fill a cocktail mixing glass three-quarters full with ice. Add the cognac, the shrub, and the lemon juice, then stir 40 times to cool. Using a Hawthorne strainer, strain the mixture into the absinthe-cured coupe glass.

Dot with my Raw Honey Aromatic Bitters, and serve to an appreciative friend. Then make another for yourself. Guests first, of course!

PUNCH AS WE KNOW IT—A FRUITY, *juicy mixture that may or may not contain booze—is a seventeenth-century import from India, and in its original form was a concoction of alcohol, sugar, water, lemon, and tea. My version is built upon a base of strong Chinese tea: I like lapsang souchong's aromatic smokiness, and it's such a good match both for Scotch and for Drambuie (which has a sort of honeyed, smoky flavor itself). Equal measures of fresh citrus juices and my Blood Orange Shrub balance things out for a tangy, spirit-lifting elixir that's sure to pep you up before your next game of croquet. A thoroughly modern examination of this quintessentially English beverage, my English Afternoon Punch will make a dozen or so of your closest friends very, very happy on a wet Saturday afternoon.*

1 750 ml bottle Blended Scotch whisky

½ 750 ml bottle Drambuie

2 cups (475 ml) Italian Blood Orange and Charred Rosemary Shrub (see page 40)

½ cup (120 ml) freshly squeezed lemon juice

½ cup (120 ml) freshly squeezed lime juice

1 quart (946 ml) seltzer water

1 quart (946 ml) Lapsang Souchong tea, strongly brewed and then cooled

20 shakes of my Cocktail Whisperer's Raw Honey Aromatic Bitters (see page 62)

Make a very large ice cube by filling a Tupperware container with spring water, then freeze. Place the ice cube into a very large punch bowl, add all the ingredients and mix well. Ladle into vintage porcelain tea cups—for all your nosy neighbors know, you're simply enjoying an abstemious cup of tea. Serves 10.

ASKEW BLOODY MARY

A TWENTIETH-CENTURY CLASSIC, *the Bloody Mary is everyone's favorite hangover cure. Originally created as a bracing, hair-raising combination of vodka, tomato juice, lemon juice, Worcestershire sauce, salt, and pepper, it's got the power to revive even the most debauched drinker after a night on the tiles. My Askew Bloody Mary is just as powerful as its predecessor, but it's far more nuanced: lightly spiced, astringent, and terribly healing. It also involves a make-in-the-shaker shrub: Combine a tomato-celery puree with a little white wine vinegar and agave syrup, add to the other ingredients in your cocktail shaker, and bang!—all the flavor of an aged shrub, whipped up in seconds. What's more, my Bloody calls for tequila instead of vodka, as well as a few drops of my Sherry Pepper Infusion for a little palate-cleansing heat—then seals the deal with vitamin C–rich lemon juice and a dose of celery bitters. Serve with a protein-rich breakfast, like an omelet stuffed with feta, spinach, and bacon.*

4 ounces (120 ml) Quick Roasted Tomato-Celery Puree (see page 155)

1/2 ounce (15 ml) white wine vinegar

1 ounce (30 ml) agave syrup

1 1/2 ounce (45 ml) *blanco* tequila, such as Casa Noble

4 drops Sherry Pepper Infusion (see page 80)

2 drops celery bitters

lemon chunks

Add all the ingredients but the bitters to a Boston shaker filled half-full with ice. Roll the shaker on an angle across the top of the bar to combine the ingredients. (You *must not* shake a Bloody Mary, ever! Shaking this elegant drink will bruise the delicate tomato fruit, and that'll yield a Bitter Mary instead of a Bloody one.) Pour the mixture over a hand-cut spear of ice into a tall Collins glass. Garnish with lemon chunks, and squeeze a little of the fresh lemon juice directly into the cocktail. Dot the celery bitters over the top to finish.

"CRANBERRY SAUCE" SHRUB

WHEN YOU SIT DOWN TO *Thanksgiving dinner, do you lunge for the big cut-glass bowl of tart, textured, homemade cranberry sauce? If your answer is yes, then this easy-to-make shrub's right up your alley. It's a distilled version of that classic New England dish, and it's redolent of cinnamon, citrus, and wintery baking spices that smell just like Christmas. Of course, unlike traditional cranberry sauce, there's no need to boil the berries to make this shrub: Here, I treat them to luxurious baths of sugar and red wine vinegar to help the fruit and spices combine and ferment. This vinegary, spice-tinged shrub needs an assertive partner, like smoky, powerful Scotch whisky.*

1 cup (110 g) cranberries,
lightly crushed

1 cup (200 g)
Demerara sugar

1 cinnamon stick

zest of 1/2 an orange

1/2 teaspoon freshly
grated nutmeg

1/2 teaspoon ground cloves

1 cup (235 ml)
red wine vinegar

TIME: 2 WEEKS. Combine the cranberries and sugar with the spices in a nonreactive bowl, and stir well to combine. Cover tightly, and let the mixture sit at cellar or fridge temperature for at least 2 days, mixing several times per day to combine the flavors. Then, pour the vinegar over the cranberry mixture and let it sit for 1 week at cellar or fridge temperature. Now, place a nonreactive sieve over another nonreactive bowl, and transfer the mixture to the sieve. Use a wooden spoon to press as much of the rich liquid through the sieve as possible. Discard the fruit pulp. Funnel the mixture into sterilized bottles or jars, and age the shrub at fridge or cellar temperature for another week or so before you use it. Use your shrub in my Cocktail Whisperer's twist on the classic Rob Roy.

MY GRANDFATHER WAS VERY FOND *of Rob Roys. He'd make them with Dewar's White Label Scotch—and that's how I knew he thought of them as a special treat, since the only spirit I'd ever seen in his house was bourbon whiskey. I'm not a big Scotch drinker myself, but even I have to admit that the Rob Roy is a woefully underrated cocktail. It's very similar to a Manhattan, only it's made with Scotch whisky instead of bourbon or rye—and it's got all the stuffing to stimulate your appetite, which makes it both a powerful aperitif and an effective digestif. So what's my Cocktail Whisperer's twist on the classic recipe? Well, I've added a portion of my Cranberry Sauce Shrub to the mix, renaming the drink, since Scotch and the perky, crisp shrub are a naturally delicious pair.*

2 ounces (60 ml)
Scotch whisky

1 ounce (30 ml) Cranberry
Sauce Shrub (see page 108)

1/4 ounce (7 ml)
sweet vermouth,
such as Carpano Antica

4 drops orange bitters

Fill a cocktail mixing glass half full with ice. Add the Scotch, the Cranberry Sauce Shrub, and the sweet vermouth. Stir gently, and then strain the mixture into a coupe glass. Dot the orange bitters over the top to finish—and lift your hat to Roy as you sip.

A TWISTED NEGRONI

THE NEGRONI HAS BEEN ON MY MIND *for years. Maybe that's because it's one of the first cocktails I ever tried—and I drank it in Rome, at the top of the famous Spanish Steps. There, in the Italian sunshine, impossibly well-dressed people were sipping short, bright-red cocktails: I quickly followed suit. And it didn't take long for me to become bewitched by the vivid Negroni. Like the bitter Italian soda I just couldn't get enough of, a Negroni tastes sharp and acerbic, and it's a classic aperitif, guaranteed to lift your palate and sharpen your appetite before a great meal. My version maintains the traditional 1:1:1 ratio of Campari, vermouth, and gin—but it benefits from the last-minute addition of dark, brooding chocolate bitters. Incredibly civilized.*

1 ounce (30 ml) Campari

1 ounce (30 ml) sweet vermouth, such as Carpano Antica

1 ounce (30 ml) London dry gin

2-3 drops chocolate bitters

Fill a cocktail mixing glass three-quarters full with ice. Add the Campari, the vermouth, and the gin, and stir gently until combined. Strain the mixture into a rocks glass, either with or without ice. Dot with the chocolate bitters, serve, and dream of a Roman holiday.

I love experimenting with craft cocktails, and creating new combinations of tastes, textures, and presentation styles. But who says all cocktails have to include booze? Not me. After all, mocktails—refreshing nonalcoholic drinks that are big on flavor—have a common ancestor: the shrub. Shrubs have an incredible facility for coaxing hidden flavors out of fruits and vegetables: no alcohol involved.

And drinkers have being doing it for centuries. I've already mentioned switchel, also known as Haymaker's Punch, a nineteenth-century non-alcoholic punch that's enjoying a major renaissance these days. A sort of "instant shrub," it's a very simple combination of vinegar, water and sweet molasses, and was very popular with laborers who were engaged in the strenuous task of making hay bales by hand. They sipped this sweet-tart non-alcoholic punch to quell their thirst and keep their hunger in check until the next meal. More importantly, using both vinegar and molasses would keep the laborers' electrolyte balances in check, which kept them from fainting from heat and dehydration. (The bosses thought the punch was a useful tool: If workers were less likely to complain about being hungry or thirsty, more work could get done.)

These days, shrubs—and bitters, too, of course—are still great tools to have at your disposal when it comes to crafting delicious booze-free cocktails. And it's important to know how to do just that. Even if you're a drinker yourself, imagine all the reasons you've had for turning down a tipple in the past. Maybe you were driving that night. Perhaps you were on medication, or maybe you were pregnant. Or, maybe you just weren't in the mood. If you're hosting a party, you can bet that at least some of your guests will be in the same boat, so they'll be delighted if you're able to offer them something more than plain old soda. And the great thing is, mocktails don't need to be less creative or exciting than their liquor-laden cousins. As the recipes in this chapter will prove to you, mocktails can be so enticing that you'll focus on their flavor, and forget about whether you're drinking alcohol or not. And what's more, they can be truly beautiful-looking drinks. Imagine the possibilities presented by colorful varieties of bitters, like crimson Peychaud's, or the burnished-orange whiskey barrel–aged variety that's available from a number of producers—or by the style of elaborate-looking but easy-to-make tiki drinks. It's official: Mocktails aren't second best to cocktails anymore. They present the drinker with handcrafted, flavor-driven refreshment—and the best part is, you can drink as many of them as you like without worrying about the morning after.

And the rules—if you can call them rules—for making mocktails are exactly the same as for their bibulous kin. Avoid soft drinks that are sweetened with corn syrup, and skip the diet soda. It's particularly important to use only freshly squeezed juices when you're creating your mocktails, since you won't be combining them with alcohol. Also, as always, be sure to use your own handmade ice. And, if you're using fresh herbs in your cocktails (and many of the recipes in this chapter, as in others, do call for them), make sure you wash and dry them well before you start making drinks. There is nothing less attractive than enthusiastically slapping your fresh, unwashed, basil, only to discover out that a nice fat grasshopper was clinging to the leaf. (Dismay is not the word.) The moral of this creepy-crawly story is, carefully pick, wash, and dry the herb, fruit, or vegetable garnishes that you plan on putting anywhere near your lovely, handcrafted drinks.

Mocktails can also benefit from a little experimentation with alternative flavors, like fire and smoke. For instance, take a small piece of fresh rosemary, and carefully light its needles on fire in a fireproof dish. Then, you can capture that smoke by holding a Boston shaker upside down over the shards

of rosemary. After that, just add some ice to your shaker and prepare your mocktail as usual. The hint of smoke left inside the shaker will swirl around the inside of the mocktail-drinker's memory for years to come. You can also try this technique with fresh sage, especially in Margarita-esque mocktails. While the recipes in this chapter don't call for smoking your herbs, you should feel free to experiment—carefully—with alternative flavors like these as the spirit takes you.

So what are we drinking? This chapter has plenty of recipes for beguiling mocktails that are sure to quench your thirst and pique your appetite. If it's hot outside, try a Mock Mint Julep, a striking combination of my Dr. Arrow's Strong Water Shrub, a little ginger beer, some English breakfast tea (really!), and spearmint. Or, make my luscious Quick Fig-Balsamic Shrub: With only three ingredients, it's quick and easy, and it's great in my Lady Frazer's Harried Excuse, an autumnal mocktail that boosts the shrub with soda water and bitters. In fact, lots of the recipes in this chapter feature palate-lifting fizzy water: take my Angostura and Seltzer Restorative, a highly effective way to put upset stomachs—or hangovers—to bed. Read on for more!

MOCK MINT JULEP

A GREAT MINT JULEP DOESN'T *need to be heavy on the booze. In fact, it doesn't really need booze at all. Say hello to my Mock Mint Julep: It's certainly one of the most exciting mocktails I've ever met. It's based on a combination of iced tea and ginger beer—but instead of simply combining them in a ⁵⁰/₅₀ ratio and calling it a day, I've added a bit of a twist in the form of my Dr. Arrow's Strong Water Shrub. That's because the shrub's beet-red hue is so striking against the clear-white crushed ice and green mint in the julep—and because it contributes a rush of flavor: think sweet beetroot, fresh lemon, and pungent spices. You'll want to drink dozens of these, and guess what? You can. (Don't tell your friends there's no booze in it; they'll be amazed by your prowess.)*

4 leaves fresh spearmint

2 ounces (60 ml) Dr. Arrow's Strong Water Shrub (see page 22)

1 ounce (30 ml) sugarcane-based ginger beer

2 ounces (60 ml) iced English breakfast tea

1 ounce (30 ml) Basic Simple Syrup (see page 152)

4 dashes Cocktail Whisperer's Raw Honey Aromatics Bitters (see page 62)

crushed ice

Place the fresh mint in a silver julep cup. Using the back of a wooden spoon, muddle the mint to release its natural oils. Add a handful of the crushed ice. Then add the Dr. Arrow's Strong Water Shrub, stir, and add another handful of ice. Now add the English breakfast tea and the ginger beer. Stir, and add a third handful of ice. Finally, add the simple syrup, and stir some more. Top with my homemade Raw Honey Aromatic Bitters. Garnish with a sprig of fresh mint and a drizzle of Dr. Arrow's Strong Water Shrub over the top for an extra burst of color and flavor. Refreshing, aromatic, and incredibly addictive.

QUICK BALSAMIC-FIG SHRUB

HERE'S ANOTHER SUMPTUOUS *quick shrub for those of you who crave instant gratification—and it's a combination that works so well in cocktails. My Quick Balsamic-Fig Shrub calls upon flavors you already know and love: Who hasn't enjoyed a salad of figs (and, perhaps, arugula) drizzled with good-quality balsamic? There's a reason it's such a good match: Fresh figs, with their sweet funkiness, are a great foil for tart, viscous balsamic vinegar. And capturing their essences in a shrub means instant success when it comes to making cocktails. This shrub would be wonderful in bourbon- or rye whiskey-based cocktails, but using booze is completely optional. You could also skip the liquor completely, and mix it with nothing more than a little soda water and a dash of simple syrup, as in the sublimely named Lady Frazier's Harried Excuse (see page 122).*

4–5 plump fresh figs, quartered

1 cup (200 g) Demerara sugar

1 cup (235 ml) balsamic vinegar

Place the fig quarters in a nonreactive bowl, and cover them with the sugar. Add the vinegar immediately, and mix well. Cover tightly, and let the mixture sit on the countertop for 2–3 days. Then, uncover the fig mixture, and mash it up a bit with a fork. Place a nonreactive strainer over another nonreactive bowl, and transfer the mixture to the strainer. Press down on the fruit mixture with a wooden spoon to squeeze out as much liquid as possible. Voila: a shrub is born. Store the mixture in a sterilized bottle or jar, and use in your mock-or cocktails immediately.

CULTIVATED BY HUMANS FOR *thousands of years, the fig figures heavily in world mythologies. Take, for instance, an anecdote mentioned in that famous study of religion and mythology, James Frazier's* The Golden Bough: *Members of Aboriginal tribes in northern Australia believed the fig-tree was the conduit by which the Sun fertilized the earth. This innovative mocktail honors Frazer's wife, who, like her husband, must have been well versed in fig-related lore—but I bet she'd never tried drinking them. She should have, since this tipple is wonderful: A brown-sugar simple syrup loosens my lush, dark, tart Quick Balsamic-Fig Shrub before it's diffused in refreshing soda water and topped with a slice of fresh fig. And it makes a great early-autumn aperitif. Serve a few rounds at your next party; it's sure to delight seasoned drinkers and teetotalers alike.*

2 ounces (60 ml) Quick Balsamic-Fig Shrub (see page 120)

1 ounce (30 ml) Demerara Sugar Simple Syrup (see page 154)

5 ounces (150 ml) soda water

slice of fresh fig

Pour the Balsamic-Fig Shrub into a Collins glass, then add the Demerara Sugar Simple Syrup. Add a spear of hand-cut ice. Top with soda water and garnish with a slice of fresh fig. (Adjust the sweetness to taste by adding a little more Demerara Sugar Simple Syrup, if necessary.)

PARSNIP, CARROT, AND FENNEL SHRUB

THIS SAVORY, ROOT-VEGETABLE-BASED *shrub is the very essence of autumn. Lightly seasoned with fresh sage and tarragon, its flavors are subtle and delicate, and patience is one of its main ingredients. Don't try to rush things here: The vegetables in my Parsnip, Carrot, and Fennel Shrub need to be chopped finely, and once* in situ *in their sugar-vinegar bath they do take several weeks to ferment—but it's all worth it in the end. Once it's ready to use, you can partner it with lightly sweetened lemonade. Or, if you feel like adding something a little stronger, know that this shrub is marvelous with gin, or even with a healthy hit of aquavit, the infamous Norwegian caraway seed–based liquor.*

3-4 cups (435-580 g) parsnips, carrots, and fennel bulb cut into small coins or chunks

2 cups (400 g) Demerara sugar

2 cups (475 ml) red wine vinegar

4 leaves fresh tarragon

4 leaves fresh sage

1 teaspoon freshly grated nutmeg

TIME: 2-3 WEEKS. Place the chopped vegetables in a wide glass bowl, cover them with the sugar, and mix well. Cover the mixture, and let it sit at cellar temperature for 2-3 days. Now add the red wine vinegar, the herbs, and the nutmeg, and mix again. Continue to let the mixture ferment at cellar temperature, stirring each day until the sugar is dissolved, and adding a little more vinegar if necessary. After 2-3 weeks, place a nonreactive strainer over a nonreactive bowl, and transfer the mixture to the strainer. Use a wooden spoon to press as much of the vegetable juice through the strainer as possible. Funnel into sterilized bottles or jars and store them in the fridge for several more weeks, shaking the bottles daily to combine and mellow the flavors.

THE THEODORE ALLEN MOCKTAIL

NAMED FOR A LARGER-THAN-LIFE *rabble-rouser, saloon owner, and criminal (Tony Soprano had nothing on him), this intriguing libation doesn't include hooch—and that's because it doesn't need any. (Unlike Allen himself, of course, who was partial to the stuff.) There's plenty of flavor in this booze-free cocktail, thanks to my Parsnip, Carrot, and Fennel Shrub: After aging for a few weeks, the parsnips' sweetness becomes more pronounced, and aromatic herbs like tarragon and sage, combined with the licorice-tinged fennel root, imbue it with subtle layers of flavor. A little lemonade and a pinch of sea salt add flavor and texture—and act as a melancholy tip-of-the-hat to the fading summer. If you ask me, mocktails made with root-vegetable-based shrubs are especially beguiling on late fall afternoons, when dusk falls early over bare trees. Go ahead and add gin here if you want to kick it Theodore Allen–style—but it's just as good* sans *liquor, if not better.*

1 ounce (30 ml) Parsnip, Carrot, and Fennel Shrub (see page 124)

2 ounces (60 ml) cool spring water

¼ ounce (7 ml) lemonade (sweetened with a little Raw Honey Simple Syrup: see page 152)

pinch of sea salt

Add the shrub to a 4 ounce (120-ml) cordial glass. Top with cool water, a drop of sweetened lemonade, and a pinch of sea salt. Sip to your heart's content, and don't be afraid to pour yourself a second round.

CUCUMBER-BASIL SHRUB

THE SCENT AND TASTE OF *freshly picked cucumbers straight off the vine is the scent and taste of high summer. When it's concentrated into a summery shrub like this one, it's even more delicious. And it goes so well with Thai basil's fresh bite (I like to use the Thai variety, since it has a bit more spice to it). That's just about all there is to my Cucumber-Basil Shrub, which is breathtakingly easy to assemble, and which matures very quickly—in only about a week. Use European-style seedless cukes to make this shrub: Slimmer and smoother-skinned, they're a slightly different beast to the usual garden-variety ones. You could use it in gin-based cocktails, or in cooling, refreshing virgin tipples, like Mr. Rankeillor's Door (opposite).*

1 European-style seedless cucumber, skin on, diced into *brunoise* (very tiny cubes)

1 small bunch fresh Thai basil

1/2 cup (100 g) Demerara sugar or Raw Honey Simple Syrup (see page 152)

1 cup (235 ml) apple cider vinegar

TIME: 1 WEEK. Combine the cucumber, basil, and sugar or sugar syrup into a nonreactive bowl and cover with the cider vinegar. Cover tightly, and let it sit in the fridge or at cellar temperature for about a week. Then, place a nonreactive strainer over a nonreactive bowl, and transfer the cucumber mixture to the strainer. Use a wooden spoon to press the mixture through the strainer, extracting as much liquid from the vegetable pulp as possible. Discard the pulp, and funnel the liquid into sterilized bottles or jars. Use liberally in craft cocktails or mocktails. (Here's a handy hint: Ran out of your favorite aftershave? Slap some of the Cucumber-Basil Shrub onto your cheeks. Seriously! It doubles as an eye-opening, alcohol-free face-freshener.)

MR. RANKEILLOR'S DOOR

FACED WITH A THIRST SO *pernicious that plain water, cocktails, sports drinks, and soft drinks all stand helpless before it? Well, help is indeed at hand, because your palate is about to become acquainted with Mr. Rankeillor's Door. Named—with good reason—for "a shrewd, ruddy, kindly, consequential man in a well-powdered wig and spectacles" from Robert Louis Stevenson's* Kidnapped, *this mocktail is just what you need to revive your spirits and sharpen your appetite for lunch. And, darn it, it's just so easy to make. Here, a flavorsome whack of my Cucumber-Basil Shrub gets pepped up with seltzer water, the barest pinch of sea salt, and my homemade bitters—and that's all there is to it. I drink Mr. Rankeillor's Doors all year round, but it really is the ticket when summer's heat is at its highest.*

2 ounces (60 ml) Cucumber-Basil Shrub (opposite)

6 ounces (180 ml) cool seltzer water

2 dashes Cocktail Whisperer's Raw Honey Aromatic Bitters (see page 62)

tiny pinch of sea salt

Add the shrub and the seltzer water to a tall Collins glass over a spear of hand-cut ice. Top with the bitters, then sprinkle the sea salt over the top of the drink.

WRINGING OUT HIS FISHERMAN'S CAP

HERE IT COMES: LEMONADE LIKE *you've never had it before. My Luscious Grilled Lemonade is about as far from the powdered stuff as you can get, and although it takes a little extra time to prepare, it's so worth it. Before juicing, you submerge your lemons in a bath of spring water, raw honey, and sea salt—and then you grill them over wood charcoal for a new, unexpected flavor. And, of course, lemon and mint are a time-honored duo, and they taste even better when you slap your mint before using it as a garnish. (Never slapped your herbs before? Start now. Simply wash a piece of spearmint well, then place it into the palm of one hand and slap your other hand against it. This releases the mint's oils and makes it cocktail-glass-ready without bruising the leaves too much.) Named for the salt-drenched headgear of hardy fishermen, this invigorating drink is lovely at lunch alongside just about anything—a burger and fries, a quinoa salad, a ham sandwich—you name it.*

4 ounces (120 ml) Luscious Grilled Lemonade (see page 152)

2 ounces (60 ml) Raw Honey Simple Syrup (see page 152)

1 ounce (30 ml) fizzy water

pinch of sea salt, then another pinch on the lemons just before grilling

fresh spearmint, slapped

pebbled ice, smashed in a Lewis bag

Combine the Grilled Lemonade and the Raw Honey Simple Syrup in a Collins glass. (Adjust sweetness to your taste, adding more Raw Honey Simple Syrup if necessary.) Add the seltzer, and a pinch of sea salt. Finish with 3-4 drops of my homemade aromatic bitters, and garnish with a few leaves of the slapped fresh spearmint.

ANGOSTURA AND SELTZER
WATER RESTORATIVE

ALL RIGHT, THE FACT IS, *you're not feeling so well this morning. You had a few drinks with the guys from work last night, usually a tame affair that has you home by nine. Last night, however, your first drink was a shot of Sambuca—and you're not sure how that happened—at the shockingly early hour of six-thirty. And things went downhill (or, perhaps, uphill?) after that. Well, as the saying goes, to be hung over is human: to recover, divine. Sufferer, meet my simple Angostura and Seltzer Water Restorative, which is* the *way to mitigate the gruesome effects of a night out on the tiles. It's so easy it can hardly be called a recipe—but I had to include it here for its sheer effectiveness. Both seltzer water and bitters are famous for their ability to subdue unruly bellies. Consuming them both at once is, to use the technical term, a double whammy of a cure. Take two, and call me in the morning.*

6 ounces (180 ml) cool seltzer water

1 teaspoon of Angostura bitters (think twice before substituting my Cocktail Whisperer's Raw Honey Aromatic Bitters: they have quite a kick!)

1 pinch sea salt

Place a spear of hand-cut ice in a Collins glass. Top with the seltzer water, add the bitters, and finish with a quick sprinkle of sea salt.

DOWN EAST MOCKTAIL

FRESH BERRIES—LIKE MY FAVORITE VARIETY, *the Maine Wild Blueberry—boast a lip-smacking acidity that's just dazzling in alcohol-free libations. With its touch of balsamic vinegar, grilled orange juice, and lush Blueberry Simple Syrup, my Down East Mocktail involves making an instant-shrub-of-sorts right in your cocktail glass—then topping the mixture up with a celebratory sparkle of seltzer water. This zesty, colorful mocktail is just the thing to whip up if you're planning, say, a festive weekend brunch, a relaxed birthday lunch, or an early-afternoon engagement party. Sometimes you just don't feel like downing mimosas or Bloody Marys before noon, so opt for a Down East instead: It's got all the jubilance of a champagne-based cocktail minus the (not-so-jubilant) aftereffects.*

1 ounce (30 ml) Blueberry Simple Syrup (see page 155)

1 teaspoon balsamic vinegar

1 ounce (30 ml) grilled orange juice (slice oranges into ½-inch rounds: grill lightly over charcoal or on a grill pan until gently colored, then juice)

seltzer water

½ inch (1.3 cm) grilled orange round, for garnish

aromatic bitters

Combine the simple syrup, vinegar, and orange juice in a champagne flute, then top with enough seltzer to fill the glass. Garnish with a round of grilled orange, and dot with the bitters.

TIKI MOCKTAIL

GET READY TO STAGE A RETURN *to the 1940s and 50s, when tiki culture reigned supreme—especially in matters of food and drink. Buy yourself a bottle of orgeat: it's a softly textured syrup that's enlivened with almonds, pure cane sugar, and either rose- or orange-flower water. In my Tiki Mocktail, it's combined with the usual tiki-esque suspects: lemon, lime, orange, and grapefruit juices, plus coconut cream and the requisite pineapple juice. But there's a twist: Toasty, smoky chicory powder adds the richness of rum to the mix, even though this drink is liquor-free. Best served alongside a grass skirt and a lei.*

1 ounce (30 ml) freshly squeezed orange juice

1 ounce (30 ml) good-quality espresso powder

1 ounce (28 g) chicory powder (kills intestinal worms, in case you were curious)

1 ounce (30 ml) freshly squeezed grapefruit juice

1 ounce (30 ml) freshly squeezed pineapple juice

1 ounce (30 ml) falernum or orgeat syrup

1 ounce (30 ml) coconut cream

½ ounce (15 ml) freshly squeezed lemon juice

½ ounce (15 ml) freshly squeezed lime juice

Cocktail Whisperer's Raw Honey Aromatic Bitters (see page 62)

fresh mint sprigs

freshly scraped nutmeg

Fill a blender half full with ice, then add all the ingredients except the bitters, mint, and the nutmeg. Blend on high for 20 seconds, and pour into tiki-style mugs. Dot the top of each drink with 2 drops of my Cocktail Whisperer's Raw Honey Aromatic Bitters, a sprig of fresh mint, and a little of the freshly grated nutmeg for a colorful, aromatic finish. Serve with a spoon, if desired. Serves 2, with a refill.

By now, you're a seasoned shrub-maker. You started out with my simple Ginger-Lime Shrub, and that's where the love affair started. Then you began to experiment. Now you've got a few shrubs maturing happily in your fridge—and the flavor combinations are all your own doing. And you've probably got a couple bottles of bitters as part of your craft cocktail kit—Peychaud's, Angostura, maybe even grapefruit bitters—and if you've really embraced your budding relationship with bitter botanicals, perhaps you've even got a big jar of my Cocktail Whisperer's Raw Honey Aromatic Bitters on your countertop, just waiting to be pressed into service in your homemade drinks. It's official: Bitters and shrubs are a big part of your mixological repertoire.

And now, it's time to take your relationship to the next level. Bitters and shrubs shouldn't be confined to the bar, because they can really work magic in the kitchen. First, allow me to introduce to you to the classic French sauce known as a gastrique. Its very name may sound ultra-elegant and sophisticated, and it is, but at the end of the day, a gastrique is simply a shrub that's produced in the kitchen over heat, and the process isn't a difficult one. Like shrubs, gastriques are combinations of vinegar, sugar, fruit, vegetables (or other flavorings), and they're usually combined in a saucepan and slowly reduced over heat until they become thick, concentrated, intensely flavored, sweet-tart syrups. (Unlike shrubs, you won't have to wait days or weeks for them to mature: about an hour is all it takes.) Then, the luscious syrup that comprises a gastrique is added to a dish as a finishing sauce—often to complement the simple, delicate, understated flavors of fresh food. It adds texture, fragrance, acidity, and intensity to pan-sautéed chicken or pork; to grilled fish; and even to fresh berries, French toast, or vanilla ice cream. That's right: gastriques can be sweet or savory—either way, adding a few drops of a well-made gastrique to just about any dish can excite your palate in a big way.

Over the years, I've experimented with all sorts of ingredients when I'm making gastriques—including peaches, apples, espresso coffee, curry powder, baking spices, plums, leeks, fresh peas, and tomatoes, and I've included lots of my favorite recipes here. And the first thing you'll notice is their simplicity. Gastriques really are a snap to make, and you don't have to be a culinary genius to put them together. If you can boil water, you can make a gastrique. The main ingredient? A little patience, since it takes about an hour for the sauce to reduce down to a nice, viscous thickness.

Wait a minute: what about bitters? I haven't forgotten them. Bring those handy little bottles into the kitchen and keep them there. Like gastriques, they add a final punch of intense flavor to lots of dishes. Since there's such a variety of bitters on the market these days—think celery, walnut, grapefruit, or even chocolate—there are bitters for just about any recipe. You can add them to soups, sauces, glazes, dressings, or even dot them onto desserts before serving. Get creative—and don't be afraid to make mistakes, since experimentation is the best way to learn.

I'm getting hungry; so let's start cooking. Have I mentioned how easy gastriques are to make? Let me say it again. They're easy. And they make for such an impressive presentation. Whip up a batch of my Basic Gastrique this weekend, and use it during the week on anything and everything: simple grilled or baked fish, light salads, or even an open-faced grilled-cheese sandwich. Next time you're craving pork chops, try my recipe, which skips the apple sauce in favor of a Maple Syrup Sazerac Gastrique. It takes its inspiration from the Sazerac cocktail, and it's nothing more than sherry wine vinegar, maple syrup, and rye whiskey, simmered until tart and toothsome. And here's where bitters come into play: A dash or two of crimson Peychaud's Bitters lends a final bite to the gastrique-laden pork. Or, if you're in the mood for dessert, look no further than my Coffee Gastrique for Vanilla Gelato. It's just a matter of heating cold, strong coffee with maple syrup, maple sugar, and vinegar until it's an irresistible syrup that's a perfect partner for vanilla ice cream. You'll also love my foolproof Broiled Grapefruit with Palm Sugar, Brandy, and Angostura Bitters. It makes a great side dish, but it's also an excellent dessert or breakfast (especially if a little hair of the dog is in order).

And there are plenty more recipes where those came from. Time to fire up the stove!

BASIC GASTRIQUE

THIS IS THE BASIC GASTRIQUE TEMPLATE, *and once you try it, you'll see how easy it is to make—and how much sparkle it adds to just about any meal. Gastriques add a unique sweet/tart zing that complements a meal's more delicate flavors, making each bite sing. Just about any dish can benefit from a well-applied gastrique: fish, chicken, pork, beef, salads—you name it. You can even drizzle it over a slice of strong cheese and enjoy after dinner alongside a glass or two of good port.*

1-2 (15–30 g) tablespoons of unsalted butter (never substitute the salted variety!)

1 shallot, finely minced

1 cup (200 g) Demerara sugar

1 cup (235 ml) apple cider vinegar

3 cups (450 g) of assorted fruits, such as citrus fruits or berries, sliced into 1/2 inch (1.3-cm) coins (or smaller)

1/4 cup (60 ml) brandy

pinch of *fleur de sel*

In a medium saucepan, melt the sweet butter over a medium heat; keep an eye on it and don't let it burn. When the butter has melted, add the shallot and cook until translucent, about 7–9 minutes. Add the sugar and let it caramelize until it's a toasty-brown color. Add the vinegar: It will splatter, so take the saucepan off the heat briefly. Replace the pan on the heat, and add the fruit and the brandy to the pan. Carefully ignite the brandy to burn off the harsh alcohol flavor, and let the mixture reduce in volume by three-quarters. Cook for 20–40 minutes, or until the fruits are quite soft. Puree the mixture in a blender, and strain before using, leaving as much or as little of the fruit pulp in the gastrique as you like. Add the pinch of *fleur de sel*. Let cool, and store in the refrigerator. This is a fragile finishing sauce with a short shelf life of about 1 week.

MAPLE SYRUP SAZERAC GASTRIQUE WITH SAUTÉED PORK CHOPS

THIS GASTRIQUE IS A *deconstructed version of the Sazerac cocktail, a combination of rye whiskey, absinthe, simple syrup, and Peychaud's Bitters that has its origins in early twentieth-century New Orleans. And it's just marvelous when drizzled over a thickly sliced pork chop that's been sautéed and then pan-roasted with potatoes and onions. The perfect balance of sweet and tart, the Maple Syrup Sazerac Gastrique is a succulent concentrate that balances the strong flavors of this hearty, comforting dish.*

FOR THE GASTRIQUE:
1 cup (235 ml) grade B (or "cooking") maple syrup

1 cup (235 ml) Spanish sherry wine vinegar

1/4 cup (60 ml) rye whiskey

1 ounce (30 ml) absinthe

FOR THE PORK CHOPS:
2 free-range pork chops, each about 2 inches (5 cm) thick

salt and pepper

1 onion, thinly sliced

1 potato, thinly sliced

Peychaud's Bitters

parsley, for garnish

To make the gastrique, add the liquid ingredients to a saucepan and, very slowly, bring them to a simmer. Simmer the mixture for 2–3 hours, stirring frequently until the sauce is thick and aromatic. Cool the gastrique and reserve. To make the pork chops, preheat your oven to 400°F (200°C, or gas mark 6). Season the meat with salt and pepper, then sear each pork chop on both side in an ovenproof sauté pan. Then add the onion and the potato to the pork chops in the pan. Place the pan in the oven and bake for 15 minutes. Remove from oven (use a heavy glove to keep from burning your hand on the pan!) and let it sit on the countertop for 2–3 minutes. Then remove the chop, onions, and potatoes from the pan, and add the gastrique to the cooking juices left over from the onions, potatoes, and pork chops. Heat this mixture, bring it to a simmer, and reduce it until it's a mere drizzle. Drip this concentrate over your pork chops, and serve with the roasted onions and potatoes. Add a couple of drops of Peychaud's Bitters to each dish for color (and healing), and garnish with fresh parsley. Serves 2.

SAUTÉED SALMON FILETS WITH AN OVEN-ROASTED TOMATO GASTRIQUE

THIS IS ONE OF THE EASIEST *and healthiest meals you'll ever make. My Oven-Roasted Tomato Gastrique, which is essentially a savory shrub, can be made well in advance, so all you'll need to do to serve it is reduce it in a saucepan with a little seasoning and lemon juice. And it takes just minutes to sauté panko-crusted salmon filets until brown, crispy, and irresistible. Serve with a side of freshly steamed asparagus for a quick-yet-sophisticated dinner.*

FOR THE GASTRIQUE:
1 pound (455 g) tomatoes, finely diced and roasted at 400˚F (200˚C, or gas mark 6) for 30 minutes, then cooled

1 cup (235 ml) apple cider vinegar

1 cup (200 g) Demerara sugar

FOR THE SALMON:
2 pounds (900 g) salmon filets, well-washed and patted dry with paper towels

flour, for dusting

salt and pepper

1 egg, beaten

1 cup (50 g) panko bread crumbs

1 tablespoon (15 ml) butter

1 tablespoon (15 ml) extra-virgin olive oil

Start to make the gastrique 1 week before you plan to use it. Combine the cooled, roasted tomatoes with the apple cider vinegar and the sugar. Cover tightly and store the mixture in a cool, dark place for about 1 week, stirring frequently. Double strain the mixture, and use in recipes that call for an oven-roasted tomato gastrique. To make the salmon, preheat your oven to 350˚F (180˚C, or gas mark 4), dust the salmon filets with flour, and season with salt and pepper. Dip each filet into the beaten egg, and roll in the panko crumbs to coat. Heat the butter and olive oil in a large ovenproof sauté pan over a medium-high heat until very hot, and sauté the salmon filets for a couple minutes on each side, until crispy. Then place the pan in the oven for another 5–7 minutes. Remove the pan from the oven (using a heavy glove to keep your hand from burning); remove the salmon from the pan and keep warm. To the same saucepan, add about an ounce or two (30–60 ml) of the tomato gastrique, reduce over a low heat to a drizzle, and season with salt, pepper, and, if you like, a squeeze of lemon. Pour this tangy sauce over the salmon, and serve.

GRAPEFRUIT AND BLOOD ORANGE GASTRIQUE WITH GRILLED DIVER SCALLOPS

TANGY BLOOD ORANGES MEET *sharply acidic grapefruit in this gorgeous gastrique that's brightly colored and brightly flavored. It's especially effective alongside seared or grilled diver scallops, where its punchy, citrusy kick brings out the scallops' natural sweetness. If all this sounds terribly complicated, let me assuage your fears: Even if you think your cooking skills are limited to pouring a bowl of cereal or boiling an egg, you'll still be able to whip up this light, delicious, summery meal—and you'll look like a pro while you're doing it. Make it tonight for someone special, and try serving it with a simple arugula salad and some crusty bread.*

FOR THE GASTRIQUE:
1/2 cup (100 g) Demerara sugar

1/4 cup (60 ml) grapefruit juice

1/2 cup (120 ml) blood orange juice or blood orange marmalade

1/2 cup (120 ml) Japanese rice wine vinegar

1/4 cup (60 ml) mirin (Japanese sweetened rice wine vinegar)

FOR THE SCALLOPS:
2 pounds (900 g) fresh diver scallops

Scallion slivers or lemon thyme leaves for garnish (optional)

To make the gastrique, add all ingredients to a small saucepan. Bring to a simmer and reduce the mixture by three-quarters. (It will look very thick.) Set aside and keep warm over a very low flame. To make the scallops, use a little oil olive on a paper towel to moisten a charcoal-fired grill. When the grill is sizzling-hot, use a pair of tongs to place each scallop on the grill, and don't move them for at least 3 minutes. Then flip them over, and sear until grill marks are visible on both sides of each scallop. To serve, use a spoon to "dot" the Blood Orange and Grapefruit Gastrique artfully on a plate. Then arrange several of the grilled scallops on top of the sauce. Finally, spoon up a little more of the gastrique, and shake or "dance" it over the top of the scallops for an extra kick. Serve with scallion slivers or a few lemon thyme leaves. So simple.

VIETNAMESE-STYLE CHICKEN SCALOPPINI WITH LAPSANG SOUCHONG GASTRIQUE

WITH ITS DISTINCTIVE FLAVORS *of smoke and whiskey, Lapsang Souchong makes a memorable gastrique. This is an elegant weeknight meal that's relatively quick to put together. Just be sure to make the gastrique a few days in advance and store it in the fridge. Serve with my Broiled Grapefruit with Palm Sugar, Brandy and Angostura Bitters—or, a little fresh, sautéed broccoli works well, too.*

FOR THE GASTRIQUE:
1 cup (235 ml) brewed Lapsang Souchong tea

2 cups (400 g) granulated cane sugar

2 tablespoons (30 ml) lemon juice

1/2 cup (120 ml) apple cider vinegar

FOR THE SCALOPPINI:
1 pound (455 g) boneless scaloppini of chicken breast (pounded flat until about 1/4 inch (.64 cm) thick)

1/2 cup (70 g) flour

salt and pepper

1 egg, beaten, plus a little water

1 cup (50 g) panko bread crumbs

5 tablespoons (75 ml) peanut oil, for frying

1 heaping tablespoon (15 g) assorted Vietnamese spices, like ground coriander, chile flakes, dried mint, and chives

1/4 ounce (60 ml) brandy

lemon juice

To make the gastrique, combine all the ingredients in a medium saucepan and simmer for about an hour, or until the mixture has reduced by about three-quarters. To make the chicken, preheat the oven to 400°F (200°C, or gas mark 6). Dredge the chicken in the flour, and season it with salt and pepper. Dip it into the egg wash, and then roll it in the panko crumbs until completely coated. Heat a cast-iron pan until it's almost smoking, then reduce the heat a bit and add the peanut oil to the pan (if you don't reduce the heat, the oil will begin to smoke). Fry the chicken scaloppini until crunchy on sides, about 4 minutes per side. Remove the pan from the heat and place in the oven for 5–7 minutes or until the juices run clear when pricked with a toothpick. Remove the chicken from the pan, sprinkle the Vietnamese-style herbs over the top and keep warm. Discard the peanut oil. Add the brandy to the pan, and carefully ignite to burn off the harsh alcohol flavor. Then add the tea gastrique to the same pan, and reduce it a little more, if necessary. Dot the gastrique around a plate, and top with the crispy chicken slices. Finish with a squeeze of lemon juice and serve immediately.

COFFEE GASTRIQUE FOR VANILLA GELATO

GOOD NEWS FOR THE SWEET-TOOTHED: *gastriques aren't just for savory dishes. It's absolutely possible to translate a gastrique into a luscious, dessert-friendly sauce that'll have your guests coming back for second—and even third—helpings. Given the chance, gelato is a welcome recipient for the concentrated flavors inherent in a gastrique, and for its trademark sweet-and-tangy finish. My Coffee Gastrique combines strong, cold coffee with a dose of maple sugar and a hint of apple cider vinegar. After letting the mixture reduce slowly, you'll have an intensely flavored finishing sauce that'll charm the socks off coffee-lovers everywhere. Serve it over the best-quality vanilla ice cream or gelato you can get your hands on for a fabulous finale to just about any meal.*

1 cup (235 ml) cold, extra-strong coffee

1 cup (200 g) maple sugar

1/4 cup (60 ml) "maple vinegar" (equal proportions of apple cider vinegar and maple syrup)

vanilla gelato or good-quality vanilla ice cream

Add all the liquid ingredients to a saucepan, and place over a medium-low heat. Reduce slowly for about an hour, or until the liquid has reduced in volume by three-quarters. Keep warm. Place two scoops of vanilla gelato or ice cream into a dish or martini glass, and spoon the Coffee Gastrique liberally over the ice cream. Tangy and delicious!

BROILED GRAPEFRUIT WITH PALM SUGAR, BRANDY AND ANGOSTURA BITTERS

GRAPEFRUIT IS JUST SO VERSATILE. *You can use it to make shrubs; you can enjoy its fresh juice in cocktails; and its tart flesh is wonderful in savory salads. But have you ever tried broiling one? It may sound weird to the uninitiated, but the fact is, grapefruit is as delicious warm as it is cold. And it goes with just about every meal. Have it for breakfast (although you might want to consider omitting the brandy and the bitters); serve it as a low-fat side dish alongside my Vietnamese-Style Chicken Scaloppini with Lapsang Souchong Gastrique; or, skip the ice cream for a change, and try it as a healthy dessert. It's a one-dish wonder, and, with only four ingredients, it's magnificently easy to whip up.*

2 pink grapefruits

2 tablespoon (30 g) palm sugar (or Demerara sugar)

2 ounce (60 ml) brandy

Angostura bitters

Slice pink grapefruits in half and place them on an ovenproof tray. Sprinkle each with 1 tablespoon (15 g) of palm or Demerara sugar and about 1 ounce (30 ml) of brandy. Broil until the sugar crust is crackling. Dash Angostura Bitters over the top, and provide a serrated spoon for easy eating. Serve the grapefruit half alongside the Vietnamese-Style Chicken Scaloppini with Lapsang Souchong Gastrique or other Asian-inspired dishes.

GRILLED CHICKEN WITH ANGOSTURA MARINADE

MOST OF THE TIME, BITTERS ARE *added to a dish just as it's about to be served. Here's a clever inversion of that rule, though: chicken that's been marinated overnight in Angostura bitters—plus onion chunks and a little fresh sage—before being tossed on the grill. It's really something to shout about. The same bold herb-and-spice-soaked flavor that adds dimension to a well-mixed Manhattan or a Rob Roy also adds depth and balance to the grilled meat. And the wonderfully charred, bitters-coated onions are a great accompaniment, too. You won't need much else: Toast some garlic bread on the grill, mix up a quick green salad, and dinner's ready.*

1 organic chicken, about 2-3 pounds (900 g-1.4 kg), cut into eighths

1 large Spanish onion, halved, then sliced

4-5 fresh sage leaves, chopped

1/4 cup (60 ml) Angostura bitters

Place the chicken, the onion pieces, and the sage in a large, nonreactive bowl, then pour the bitters over them. Stir to coat well. Cover and refrigerate overnight. The next day, prepare a charcoal or gas fire. Only light one side, leaving the other side cool to create convection. Place the Angostura Bitters–marinated chicken and onions over the hot side of the grill with the top on and the air holes on the top nearly closed. (Open them on the bottom of your grill, however.) Cook the chicken over the flame for 2-3 minutes, flip, and move it to the cool side of the grill. Close the lid and do not open it again for 50 minutes. To test doneness, prick the thighs and the deepest part of the breast. When the juices run clear the bird is cooked. Remove the chicken and the onions from the grill and set into a 250°F (120°C, or gas mark 1/2) oven for approximately 10 minutes without touching! Serve with a tall glass of seltzer with a few hits of Angostura—purely for health reasons, of course!

MANGO, CURRY, AND LIME GASTRIQUE WITH HALIBUT

IF YOU'VE HAD MANGO IN SAVORY *dishes before, you already know how well its sumptuous flavor symphonizes with assertive flavors: if not, you're about to learn! Mango is particularly good in curries—its cooling sweetness takes the edge off their fiery spice—hence the inspiration for this fish-friendly Mango, Curry, and Lime Gastrique. I like to match it with halibut, which has a firm, dense flesh and works so well on the grill, but you can replace it with just about any other meaty, white-fleshed fish, such as monkfish or scallops. Serve the gastrique-dotted fish with jasmine rice and sautéed fresh green vegetables, like snow peas.*

FOR THE GASTRIQUE:
1 cup (200 g) Vietnamese palm sugar

1 cup (235 ml) sherry wine vinegar

1 cup (165 g) cubed mango (be sure that the mango is very ripe)

2 ounces (60 ml) freshly squeezed lime juice

2 teaspoons (10 g) curry powder

FOR THE HALIBUT:
2 halibut filets, ½ pound (225 g) each

To make the gastrique, place the palm sugar in a medium saucepan over a low heat. Cook slowly, raising the heat as the sugar begins to melt. When the sugar begins to caramelize—it'll be the same color as brown sugar—remove the pan from the heat and slowly add the sherry wine vinegar. (It'll splatter wildly, so have a bowl of ice and water handy to plunge your hand into in case some of the molten sugar hits your skin: Caramelized sugar sticks and burns.) Add the cubed mango. Place back on a medium heat, then add the lime juice and the curry powder. Stir to combine with a whisk. Reduce the mixture to a very thick liquid, strain, and let cool. To make the halibut, heat a cast-iron griddle until smoking hot. Place the halibut on the hot griddle and grill 5 minutes per side. To serve, use a spoon to dot the gastrique on a plate. Top with the halibut filet, and drizzle a little more gastrique onto the fish. Serves 2.

TWO: IT'S A MAGIC NUMBER. *Here, two very basic ingredients—balsamic vinegar and palm sugar—partner up to make one of the world's most versatile gastriques. You can drip this lip-licking elixir over fresh strawberries, or drizzle it over hunks of aged Parmesan; or you can even take it by the tablespoonful, as an antidote to stomach cramps. (Don't knock it till you've tried it!) I've even been known to use this Balsamic Vinegar Gastrique in cocktails: I like to add it to my Manhattans—much to the distress of purists everywhere, I'm sure. And it's a hit when it's dripped over chicken thighs that have been spread with Thai chile paste and roasted alongside tangerines—a sweet, tangy, spicy, comforting dish.*

FOR THE GASTRIQUE:
1 cup (200 g) palm sugar

1 cup (235 ml) balsamic vinegar

FOR THE CHICKEN THIGHS:
2–4 pounds (900 g–1.8 kg) bone-in, skin-on chicken thighs

1/2 teaspoon (3.5 g) Thai chile paste

3 tangerines, peeled and sectioned

4 shallots, peeled and ends trimmed

1 whole bulb of garlic, top 1/3 of bulb sliced off

To make the gastrique, add the palm sugar to a sauté pan. Heat over a medium heat until a brown, liquidy caramel begins to form. Remove the pan from the heat and pour in the balsamic vinegar. Place back on medium heat and reduce to desired thickness. To make the chicken thighs, preheat your oven to 400°F (200°C, or gas mark 6). Rub the chicken thighs the with Thai chile paste (adding a little more to taste if you like). Place the tangerine sections in an ovenproof dish, then place the chicken thighs in a single layer on top of the tangerine segments, and nestle the shallots and garlic between the chicken and the tangerine pieces. Roast for 20 minutes at 400°F (200°C, or gas mark 6), then reduce the temperature to 300°F (150°C, or gas mark 2), and roast for another 40 minutes. To serve, slice the succulent meat away from the bone, and drizzle the balsamic gastrique over it.

RED BERRY DESSERT GASTRIQUE

THIS FRUIT-LADEN GASTRIQUE IS SO *simple to make that you can hardly call it a recipe—but I just had to include it here, since it's one of my favorite ways to pull dessert together in an instant. My Red Berry Dessert Gastrique is a foolproof way to gussy up just about anything sweet, from flourless chocolate cake to fresh fruit to plain old vanilla ice cream. Even though it's made from pureed red berries, I like to drizzle it over more fresh, whole red berries—whatever's in season—for a healthy finish to a warm-weather meal, like my Sautéed Salmon Filets with an Oven-Roasted Tomato Gastrique (see page 141). And, in case you're having trouble finding it, pomegranate vinegar is available in most Middle Eastern or Asian markets.*

1 cup (200 g) raw cane sugar

½ cup (120 ml) pomegranate vinegar

1 cup (150 g) pureed red fruits, such as strawberries, raspberries, and/or cherries

Combine all the ingredients in a small saucepan. Bring to a boil, then reduce the heat and simmer for 10–20 minutes, or until the mixture has reached the desired thickness. Strain the fruit mixture, and let cool. To serve, place a couple handfuls of fresh, assorted red berries into a small glass bowl or martini glass. Drizzle the gastrique over the berries, and serve to your very, very happy guests. If you're a chocoholic—and who isn't? —you can serve it alongside homemade brownies. Or, melt a couple tablespoons of good-quality dark chocolate, and spoon it over the berries. Simple!

SYRUPS AND INFUSIONS

BASIC SIMPLE SYRUP

Add 1 cup (235 ml) of boiling water to 1 cup (200 g) of bar sugar or caster sugar and mix until sugar has dissolved. Let the mixture cool. Keep refrigerated in an airtight container for up to a month.

RAW HONEY SIMPLE SYRUP

Add 1 cup (235 ml) of boiling water to 1 cup (340 g) raw honey and mix until honey has dissolved. Let the mixture cool. Keep refrigerated in an airtight container for up to a month.

HOMEMADE LEMONADE

Warm 10 cups (2.4 L) of spring water in a large saucepan until just below simmering. Then add 1 cup (340 g) raw honey, and stir until dissolved. Let cool. Add the juice of 8 lemons. Pour the mixture into a large pitcher, and add a big handful of fresh mint. Chill in the refrigerator for a few hours before serving. (Do not add ice directly to the lemonade.)

LUSCIOUS GRILLED LEMONADE

Remove the wax from 8 lemons, and cut them into 1/2 inch (1.3-cm) rounds. Combine 1/2 cup (170 g) raw honey and 1/2 cup (120 ml) water in a bowl, and dip the lemon rounds into the mixture. Sprinkle the lemon rounds with a pinch of sea salt, then char them lightly over indirect heat on a wood grill. Let them cool, then juice them and follow the directions for my Homemade Lemonade, above.

ROASTED STRAWBERRIES AND RHUBARB

First, hull 1 pound (455 g) of strawberries, and wash 1 pound (455 g) of rhubarb stalks. Chop the rhubarb into 1 inch (2.5-cm) chunks. Preheat your oven to 400°F (200°C, or gas mark 6), and place the fruit into a cast-iron roasting pan. Roast for 30 minutes, then reduce the temperature to 300°F (150°C, or gas mark 2) and continue to roast for another 30 minutes. Let cool. Store in an airtight container in the refrigerator for up to a week.

CAPTAIN SILVER'S QUICK CELERY PICKLE

Wash a package of organic celery well, and change the water several times to eliminate any clinging grit. Trim the celery and cut it into small coins. Combine 1/2 cup (120 ml) mirin, 1/2 cup (120 ml) rice wine vinegar, and 1 cup (200 g) of Vietnamese palm sugar: this should be enough to cover the celery. (Add a few slivers of Thai chilies for extra flavor, if you like.) Add 1 teaspoon of black peppercorns, smashed with the side of a chef's knife, and 2–3 lemon zest twists. Cover and refrigerate for 2 days, stirring the mixture daily to ensure that the celery is covered with liquid, and adding more mirin if necessary. Store in an airtight container in the refrigerator for 1 month.

MUSCOVADO SUGAR SIMPLE SYRUP

Add 1 cup (235 ml) of boiling water to 1 cup (200 g) of muscovado sugar and mix until sugar has dissolved, adding a little extra water if the mixture looks too thick. Let the mixture cool. Keep refrigerated in an airtight container for up to a month.

DEMERARA SUGAR SIMPLE SYRUP

Add 1 cup (235 ml) of boiling water to $1/2$ cup (100 g) of Demerara sugar and mix until sugar has dissolved. Let the mixture cool. Keep refrigerated in an airtight container for up to a month.

BOSC PEAR "SHRUB" SIMPLE SYRUP

Finely dice 2 Bosc pears, and combine them with 1 cup (235 ml) Basic Simple Syrup (see page 152), $1/2$ cup (120 ml) Japanese rice wine vinegar and $1/2$ cup (120 ml) mirin. Add to a small saucepan, and bring to a simmer, then remove from heat, let cool, cover, and let the mixture sit overnight at cellar temperature. Strain, then use in your shrub.

HOMEMADE GRENADINE SYRUP

Combine 1 cup (235 ml) pomegranate juice, 1 cup (235 ml) Basic Simple Syrup (see page 152), and 1 cup (235 ml) freshly squeezed lemon juice, and reduce the mixture over a low heat until it reaches the desired thickness. Let cool. Add an extra 1–2 tablespoons freshly squeezed lemon juice and a bit of freshly grated nutmeg, if you like. Keep refrigerated in an airtight container for up to a month.

EASY HOME-CURED COCKTAIL CHERRIES

Add 1 pound (455 g) pitted Ranier or dark cherries to a large, sterilized Mason jar. Cover the cherries with a combination of bourbon and green tea in a ratio of 60% bourbon and 40% green tea. Refrigerate for a month. Store in the refrigerator nearly indefinitely.

QUICK ROASTED TOMATO-CELERY PUREE

Preheat your oven to 400°F (200°C, or gas mark 6). Slice about 12 ripe tomatoes, and cut the stalks from a package of well-washed celery into coins. Drizzle a little olive oil over the tomatoes and celery, sprinkle them with sea salt, and roast for 1 hour. Let the vegetables cool, and then puree them in a blender.

SPICY PICKLED CUCUMBER GARNISH

Slice a European cucumber lengthwise. Combine with 1/2 cup (120 ml) white vinegar, a few shards of sliced red chiles, 1 tablespoon (15 g) sugar, and 1 teaspoon sea salt. Cover tightly and store in the fridge overnight. Pour off the marinade, and use the pickled cucumber slices as garnishes for your cocktails.

BLUEBERRY SIMPLE SYRUP

Simply puree 1 pint (300 g) of blueberries (preferably Maine wild blueberries, if you can get them), then sweeten to taste with Raw Honey Simple Syrup (see page 152). Let cool. Store in the refrigerator for 1 month.

QUICK RAW HONEY BITTERS

Simply combine 1 1/2 cups (510 g) raw honey with 1 cup (235 ml) aromatic bitters (such as Angostura). Let the mixture steep for 24 hours. Strain, then transfer to a sterilized bottle or jar. Store unrefrigerated, nearly indefinitely.

How To Sterilize a Bottle: Using a pair of rubber-coated metal tongs, submerge the bottle in boiling water for 2 minutes. Remove the bottle, empty it of water, and let cool.

ACKNOWLEDGMENTS

I'M ACKNOWLEDGING the bartending community around the globe for putting the capital H in hospitality. To my wife, Julie, for that whoopee pie recipe in Whiskey Cocktails and for helping me follow my dreams.

TO ANN TUENNERMAN, founder of Tales of the Cocktail, for being an important guide in my professional career when no one else really offered to teach me anything. I try to follow her example for simplicity.

TO LAURA BADDISH, for calling me a mensch and being so kind. To Hanna Lee, for offering to do so much when I could never afford to do much in return--other than say thank you.

TO GARY REGAN, for even noticing me.

And to many others who aren't surprised that I don't work in private banking any longer.

What a long strange trip it's been!

ABOUT THE AUTHOR

WARREN BOBROW IS THE FOOD AND DRINK editor of
Wild River Review, in Princeton, New Jersey. He was one of twelve
journalists worldwide, and the only one from the United States, to
participate in the Fête de la Gastronomie, held September 2012, in the
Burgundy region of France. He attends Tales of the Cocktail and The
Manhattan Cocktail Classic yearly. Warren is the former owner and
cofounder of Olde Charleston Pasta in Charleston, South Carolina,
while cooking at the Primerose House and Tavern (also in Charleston).
He has published over 300 articles on everything from cocktail
mixology to restaurant reviews to travel articles. Warren was # 30 in
Saveur magazine's 100 in 2010 for his writing about the humble tuna
melt. He also writes for the "Fabulous Beekman 1802 Boys" as their
cocktail writer (Klaus, the Soused Gnome). You may find Warren on
the Web at www.cocktailwhisperer.com

X INDEX

INDEX